Teach, Flourish, Thrive

The Burnout-Busting Teachers' Journal

Rowena Hicks

Platypus Publishing

CONTENTS

ACKNOWLEDGMENTS

To my four inspiring, amazing and thoughtful children. Abs, Leah, Jack and Jamie. I am forever grateful for your belief in me and for loving me despite my mess ups! I love you all more than I can say!

Thanks too for the expertise of Martin, Divya, Jess and Tammy. Without you all, this book wouldn't be the finished article!

I thank God for His love and inspiration.

ABOUT THE AUTHOR

Rowena Hicks

Rowena Hicks has worked in education for over thirty years. First as a teacher then as a special needs coordinator, trainer and deputy headteacher. Throughout her journey in many schools, Rowena Hicks has had the chance to work with amazing teachers and teaching assistants who always put the students first, often at the expense of their own well-being.

Balancing long work hours with raising four children led Rowena to experience burnout. She now supports school staff to manage the pressures of school life and even to thrive in the midst of it.

Her passion is to work with staff to reignite their passion for teaching, to find energy and fulfilment again. Rowena has seen too many teachers lose their confidence and forget their immense value. She is here to remind them of their strengths and the incredible impact they have on their students lives.

INTRODUCTION

Welcome to Your Journaling Journey

Welcome to your journey toward discovering your best self, amidst a busy and crucial role. This 52-week journal is designed to help you beat burnout and thrive both inside and outside of school.

Why I Wrote It

I found being a teacher incredibly rewarding but sometimes overwhelming. The daily pressures, responsibilities and sheer volume of work led me to experience significant stress and burnout.

In my 30+ years of being a teacher and school leader, I experienced burnout first-hand. The passion I had for my roles never waned, but I neglected to care for myself. Long hours, people-pleasing, over-conscientiousness, and poor boundaries took their toll. Subconsciously, I believed my value came from success, achievement, and affirmation; I constantly strived to do more.

Does any of this resonate with you?

Despite the challenges, there were positives: my four incredible children became highly independent and better cooks than me! I helped numerous families, children, and colleagues over the years. Now, my mission is to support those in education to think, speak, and act differently, to have more energy, productivity, creativity, and a better work-life balance, hopefully rediscovering the joy of the role.

I have always journaled but without direction or support. Since experiencing burnout, I have learned to journal more creatively. This journal is the product of my personal growth, research, and much-needed help from others.

Craig Groeschel says, "Successful people do consistently what other people do occasionally." Hold on to this as you slowly build the habits you want and need.

What You Will Find

In this journal, you will find tools, reflections, and exercises for the next 52 weeks to help you manage stress and find joy in your teaching journey. Each week includes prompts, activities, and tips crafted specifically to support your mental, physical, and emotional well-being.

I hope you will be challenged, inspired, and motivated to grow, learn, and become the best version of yourself for both you and your family.

How to Use This Journal

- **Consistency is key**: Set aside a few minutes each day to write in your journal. This small but consistent practice can lead to significant positive changes over time.
- **Be honest and kind**: Approach your entries with honesty and self-compassion. This is a judgment-free zone where you can express your true feelings and experiences.
- **Reflect and revisit**: Periodically review your past entries to observe your growth and progress. This reflection can be profoundly encouraging and enlightening.

Remember, this journal is about YOU. It's here to support you in becoming the best version of yourself, both as an educator and as an individual. Embrace each page with an open heart and mind, and let this journey rejuvenate your spirit and reignite your passion for teaching.

At the end of the journal, you will find blank pages for when your thoughts overflow and bonus pages for when you need something extra or different – perhaps a reminder of your value, or an idea of how to plan your week using a life planner so you put your needs first.

Need Help?

Consider suggesting to one or two colleagues that they join you on this journey. Discussing your experiences can build accountability, make the process more enjoyable, and strengthen relationships.

Alternatively, join our Facebook group to share your progress and connect with others who are committed to learning and growing in their habits, outlook, and mindset. Join the Facebook Group: https://www.facebook.com/groups/preventingteacherburnout

Top Tips

- Remember that this is for your eyes only.
- Keep it short to start with, until you find the best time to fit it into your day.
- This journal is for those serious about growing and developing their skills, outlook, productivity, responses, and self-awareness - be prepared to be challenged and inspired!
- There is no right way to approach the weeks - they don't have to be completed in order!

Benefits to you

Journaling has been shown to reduce stress, boost mental clarity, and promote overall well-being. By committing to this practice, you're not only supporting your mental health but also enhancing your capacity to nurture your students and colleagues.

Commencing this journal is a commitment to self-care and a declaration that your health and happiness matter. I am thrilled you are embarking on this journey of journaling. Let's get going on this 52-week adventure together and nurture the incredible teacher within you.

Remember to start being kinder to yourself. This is a good step! Have fun.

PS – for more depth on some of these ideas, try reading my book. www.rowenahicks.com

"You are allowed to be both a masterpiece and a work in progress simultaneously." Sophia Bush

JOURNAL CONTENT CHECKLIST

WEEK	THEME	COMPLETE
1	Foundations of success	☐
2	Building blocks of habits and mindset	☐
3	Action against unhealthy habits and mindsets	☐
4	What does mental fitness look like?	☐
5	Are boundaries really necessary?	☐
6	Awareness: the key to growth	☐
7	What is the 5:1 juggle?	☐
8	Self-care strategy week	☐
9	What's my contribution?	☐
10	What about me?	☐
11	Transformative self-talk	☐
12	Kindness to yourself and others	☐
13	Do vulnerability and humility feel like a good idea?	☐
14	Do you know your value?	☐
15	Adapt to thrive: the power of teachability	☐

WEEK	THEME	COMPLETE
16	Celebrating Small steps	
17	Unseen no more: recognising your worth	
18	Building resilience	
19	Juggling	
20	Overcoming people pleasing	
21	Effortless routines, endless energy	
22	Decision fatigue	
23	One new skill to build confidence	
24	Rest in the rush	
25	Fuelling your best self: the power of nutrition and hydration	
26	Distraction detox	
27	Steady pulse: strategies to regulate emotions effectively	
28	Navigating rough waters: finding strength amidst challenges	
29	Daring to be myself	
30	Clear the clutter	

WEEK	THEME	COMPLETE
31	Finding laughter and joy	☐
32	Changing the conversation	☐
33	Retraining mind and body	☐
34	Together we thrive: cultivating awareness for others	☐
35	Practical steps to take when overwhelmed	☐
36	Recognising your strengths	☐
37	Pathways to purpose: reflecting on our choices	☐
38	My impact!	☐
39	Organise, prioritise, achieve!	☐
40	Cultivating a sense of enough: embracing adequacy	☐
41	The many faces of school relationships	☐
42	How to sync work and life	☐
43	Stress busting!	☐
44	Longer holiday	☐
45	Surviving holiday havoc	☐
46	Unplug, unwind and recharge	☐

WEEK	THEME	COMPLETE
47	A week off…phew!	☐
48	Last week of the holidays	☐
49	Start of the holidays	☐
50	Help, I can't switch off!	☐
51	Writing a new story for myself!	☐
52	What I've learnt…..so far!	☐

WEEK - 1
FOUNDATIONS OF SUCCESS

Monday

Date:_____

First thing (or Sunday evening)**:**

What is one goal I can set myself for this week that will demonstrate to myself that I am putting myself first?

e.g. exercise, journaling, time with friends, reading, eating healthy food……

_____

_____

_____

What four things or people am I grateful for today? Why?

_____

_____

_____

_____

Tip: Book it into my diary so it can't be squeezed out!

End of the day:

What was my biggest win or positive impact I had?

_____

_____

_____

Something I learnt today:

_____

_____

_____

Do you understand your self-worth? Once you do, you become a better version of yourself.
Rowena Hicks

www.rowenahicks.com/books

Date:_____

First thing:

What one thing went well yesterday?

_____

_____

_____

_____

What one thing can I complete so that at the end of the day I can congratulate myself that I DID IT?

_____

_____

_____

Tip: Choose that task you have been putting off and see how it feels to actually get rid of it!

End of the day:

Did I manage to complete that task (I'd been putting off)? Did I take a step towards completing it? How does that feel?

_____

_____

_____

_____

What am I grateful for today?

1_____

2_____

3_____

Our value doesn't come from our success or our material possessions. It comes from our character, our actions and the positive impact we have on others and the world around us.
Anonymous

https://www.facebook.com/groups/preventingteacherburnout

Wednesday

Date:_____

First thing:

One thing I can do today to get more healthy is:

_____

_____

_____

_____

One person I can reach out to today who needs a little encouragement is:

_____

_____

_____

Tip: Today I will log the WINS in my day, both big and small!

End of the day:

Who have I supported, helped or encouraged today? How did both they and I feel as a result:

_____

_____

_____

_____

Three people I'm grateful for today? Why?

1_____

2_____

3_____

Going solo to shine your light is powerful, but going together as a beacon illuminates the limitless potential in each other. Be the spark that ignites those around you.
Jim Kwik.

Thursday

Date:_____

First thing:

What am I most grateful for today?

_____

_____

_____

_____

What is my best habit that I could focus on today to keep me balanced?

_____

_____

_____

Tip: Watch my self-talk today! Am I giving myself the advice I'd give a friend?

End of the day:

Today I felt at my best when…? Why was this? Can I repeat it tomorrow?

_____

_____

_____

What did I learn today about myself?

1. A positive -

_____

_____

2. An area I can work on getting better at -

_____

_____

There is nothing noble in being superior to your fellow man; true nobility is being superior to your former self.
Ernest Hemingway

Friday

Date:_____

First thing:

What do I consider my most valued / valuable strengths? (At least three!)

_____

_____

_____

Dare I ask three trusted colleagues or friends what they see as my main strengths that they value?

_____

_____

_____

Tip: Watch today for when I felt good about myself and how things are going. Am I using my valued strengths?

End of the day:

Note one point in my day when I started to feel a moment of flow, even a short time. What was I doing?

_____

_____

_____

_____

What was the most important thing I did today? Why was it important to me?

_____

_____

_____

_____

My circumstances don't define me, my choices and responses do!
Anonymous

https://www.facebook.com/groups/preventingteacherburnout

Weekend

Date:_____

First thing:

This term, so far, I'm most proud of:

_____

_____

_____

_____

Describe a challenge I'm facing right now. What is one small step I could take to address it?

_____

_____

_____

Tip: Ask myself daily "What is one good thing to be thankful for today?"

End of the day:

What am I most grateful for this weekend?

1_____

2_____

3_____

4_____

How am I doing with the goal I set on Monday? Can I see progress?

_____

_____

_____

_____

Vulnerability is not weakness; it's our greatest measure of courage.
Brené Brown

WEEK - 2

BUILDING BLOCKS OF HABITS AND MINDSET

Monday

Date:_____

First thing:

What am I most grateful for today?

_____

_____

_____

_____

What habit can I start this week that will remind me to prioritise myself?

_____

_____

_____

Tip: Small acts of self-care can help replenish your energy and reduce stress.

End of the day:

Where did I make a difference today?

_____

_____

_____

_____

What was the most important thing I did today? Why was it important to me?

_____

_____

_____

_____

Change the way you look at things and the things you look at change.
Wayne Dwyer

Tuesday

Date:_____

First thing:

Remember one reason I went into teaching. What inspired me to start this journey?

_____

_____

_____

_____

What are three best moments of my teaching career that spring to mind?

_____

_____

_____

Tip: Watch today for when I have a positive impact on a child or a colleague.

End of the day:

What was the biggest win/positive impact I had?

_____

_____

_____

_____

What was an interaction with a colleague or student that impacted the other person today?

_____

_____

_____

_____

Education is the most powerful weapon which you can use to change the world.
Nelson Mandela

Wednesday

Date:_____

First thing:

Today I decide I can beat the to-do list. What is one task I can complete to reduce it substantially? Perhaps the one I've been putting off?

_____

_____

_____

_____

Three people who have helped and supported me recently. How?

_____

_____

_____

Tip: Prioritise that goal and make it happen today!

End of the day:

Did my day go as planned today? What can I adapt for tomorrow?

_____

_____

_____

_____

Three people I have helped today? How were they impacted?

_____

_____

_____

_____

Taking care of yourself is an act of self-respect and self-empowerment.
Unknown

Thursday

Date:_____

First thing:

Who in my team needs a kind word, note or smile?

_____

_____

_____

_____

What is one task that I could ask for help with, or work on together with a colleague?

_____

_____

_____

Tip: One step at a time - even small victories make a difference!

End of the day:

Did I impact a colleague with an act of kindness? How do I feel about that? How did they respond?

_____

_____

_____

_____

What did I contribute to my team today? Strengths, time, resources, encouragement - be honest with myself!

_____

_____

_____

_____

Collaboration is the foundation of great achievements.
Unknown

https://www.facebook.com/groups/preventingteacherburnout

Friday

Date:_____

First thing:

What is one achievement I'm proud of today, and one from this week:

_____

_____

_____

_____

How does my body feel this morning? Can I relax my shoulders? Face? Jaw?

_____

_____

_____

Tip: Focus on what you have achieved and the struggles take second place.

End of the day:

Thoughts about my week:

_____

_____

_____

_____

Where did I see or feel joy this week? Can I think of three times? When and why?

_____

_____

_____

_____

Vulnerability is the birthplace of innovation, creativity and change.
Brené Brown

Weekend

Date:_____

First thing:

What are six words that describe my day or my week?

Happy, sad, frustrated, angry, delighted, exhausted, energetic, inspired, celebrating, shocked, thoughtful, upside-down, worried, frazzled, no idea…other

_____

_____

_____

What is one positive action step I can take to improve one of these emotions? Can I ask someone to help?

_____

_____

Tip: This weekend, try time chunking, booking in time for ME.

End of the day:

List here where I have prioritised myself today. What did this look like? What worked to help me relax and unwind?

_____

_____

_____

_____

One goal I am setting myself for next week to show myself I have value:

_____

_____

_____

_____

The only thing standing between you and your goal is the story you keep telling yourself as to why you can't achieve it.
Jordan Belfort

https://www.facebook.com/groups/preventingteacherburnout

WEEK - 3
ACTION AGAINST UNHEALTHY HABITS AND MINDSETS

Monday

Date:_____

First thing: (or Sunday evening):

What is one goal I can set for this week to break an unhealthy habit?
e.g. leaving work half an hour earlier, take a lunch break, eat healthy snacks, don't work for the hour before bed.

_____

_____

_____

What words best describe how I feel about this week? Why?

_____

_____

_____

Tip: Focus on positive things booked in, positive people, each WIN!

End of the day:

What was the biggest win/positive impact I had today?

_____

_____

_____

_____

Something I learnt today:

_____

_____

_____

_____

Success is not the key to happiness. Happiness is the key to success. If you love what you are doing, you will be successful.
Albert Schweitzer

https://www.facebook.com/groups/preventingteacherburnout

Tuesday

Date:_____

First thing:

How am I feeling as I get up today? What words describe ME right now?

_____

_____

_____

_____

Now focus on my strengths, things I know I am good at:

_____

_____

_____

_____

Tip: Watch today for the WINS in my day. What do I contribute to others?

End of the day:

Describe two wins or times I made a positive impact:

_____

_____

_____

_____

Which five things or people am I grateful to have in my life right now:

_____

_____

_____

_____

Vulnerability is not weakness; it's our greatest measure of courage.
Brené Brown

https://www.facebook.com/groups/preventingteacherburnout

Wednesday

Date:_____

First thing:

What am I looking forward to today?

_____

_____

_____

_____

What am I not looking forward to today? Be aware of my regulation and breathe to be calm. Does it help, or does something else help?

_____

_____

_____

Tip: Watch my Window of Tolerance. Can I stay within my optimal area?

End of the day:

Did my day go as planned today? When did I succeed in staying regulated or not? How can I be better at this tomorrow?

_____

_____

_____

_____

My two best moments today - why did they make me buzz?

_____

_____

_____

_____

You are imperfect, you are wired for struggle, but you are
worthy of love and belonging.
Brené Brown

Thursday

Date:_____

First thing:

What is a moment I can take in my day to be kind to myself? Can I share it with a colleague?

_____

_____

_____

Who do I know in school who is really struggling, that I can clock in with today?

_____

_____

_____

Tip: One step at a time - even small victories make a difference!

End of the day:

How did I feel when I went to check on a struggling colleague? How did they respond?

_____

_____

_____

_____

Three examples today where I was kind to myself. Did I manage three?

_____

_____

_____

_____

The best way to find yourself is to lose yourself in the service of others.
Mahatma Gandhi

https://www.facebook.com/groups/preventingteacherburnout

Friday

Date:_____

First thing:

Which of the children in my class/es is thriving right now and who am I worried about? Choose two of each:

_____

_____

_____

_____

What is one thing I can put in place for each of these?

_____

_____

_____

Tip: Watching the progress of others and our role in this, we gain joy!

End of the day:

How did the children respond to my efforts and input? How did I feel? We succeed and we fail, but in all things we grow!

_____

_____

_____

_____

One tiny thing that went right today:

_____

_____

_____

_____

The meaning of life is to find your gift. The purpose of life is to give it away.
Pablo Picasso

https://www.facebook.com/groups/preventingteacherburnout

Date:_____

First thing:

What was my greatest achievement this week? Home, school, relationship, self-care?

_____

_____

_____

Did I manage to take steps to break that habit from the start of the week? What worked or didn't? Is there a small change I can make for next week?

_____

_____

_____

Tip: Self-care day! Prioritise yourself and see what happens!

End of the day:

List here where I have prioritised myself today. What did this look like? What worked to help me relax and unwind?

_____

_____

_____

_____

If I am running on empty, can I list three things that can fill my tank for the next day or two? Remember, I have to take action and make them happen!

_____

_____

_____

Self-care is giving the world the best of you, instead of what's left of you.
Katie Reed

https://www.facebook.com/groups/preventingteacherburnout

WEEK - 4
WHAT DOES MENTAL FITNESS LOOK LIKE?

Monday

Date:_____

First thing:

What might a mental fitness week look like? Can I agree to try to swap some thoughts, words and actions? What do I commit to trying?
e.g. changing self-talk to see positives, opportunities, responses, try something I haven't done before….

_____

_____

_____

What is a hurdle I have to jump over this week? How can I beat it? What might help me feel it is achievable?

_____

_____

_____

Tip: Watch my self-talk. Ban I CAN'T words.

End of the day:

What worked today? Where did I show even a small step of mental fitness today? What was the impact on me or others?

_____

_____

_____

_____

What is one thing I thought I couldn't do recently, that I now can?

_____

_____

_____

_____

Strength doesn't come from what you can do. It comes from overcoming the things you once thought you couldn't.
Rikki Rogers

https://www.facebook.com/groups/preventingteacherburnout

Tuesday

Date:_____

First thing:

Catch the thoughts going through my mind right now. Are they overwhelmed? Positive? Hopeful? Be honest!

_____

_____

_____

How can I turn even one negative thought into a positive?

e.g. "I can't do this" becomes "I'm going to ask a colleague to help me with that task".

_____

_____

_____

Tip: Watch each thought today, capture it, redirect your focus, and say "NO. I CAN DO THIS." (I might need help, but remember how much I enjoy being asked to help others!)

End of the day:

Describe two times today when something turned out well that I wasn't expecting:

_____

_____

_____

_____

Five things I'm looking forward to in the next week:

_____

_____

_____

_____

Your mind is a powerful thing. When you fill it with positive thoughts, your life will start to change.
Unknown

https://www.facebook.com/groups/preventingteacherburnout

Wednesday

Date:_____

First thing:

How is my confidence today? Do I have an opportunity to remind myself of my skills and strengths? Where and when might this be?

_____

_____

_____

What do I have to do today that feels like a drain on my energy and resources? How can I turn it on its head, so it becomes an opportunity to make a difference? Try it with something small. Do I dare try?

_____

_____

_____

Tip: Is your glass full, empty or a glass of opportunity?

End of the day:

Did my day go as planned today? Did I find an opportunity that turned out to be different as I approached it from another angle?

_____

_____

_____

_____

What are two times today I did a really GREAT job?

_____

_____

_____

_____

Believe in yourself and all that you are. Know that there is something inside you that is greater than any obstacle.
Christian D. Larson

https://www.facebook.com/groups/preventingteacherburnout

(Chapter 6 for more information on that glass!)

Thursday

Date:_____

First thing:

How am I feeling about my relationships at home and school today?
What words best describe my five key connections?

_____

_____

_____

Is there a colleague or friend I could check in with today whom I find a bit
challenging to connect with? If this could build trust, hope, and a
stronger team, who would it be and how can I approach them?

_____

_____

_____

**Tip: Remember I am only responsible for my own responses, not those
of others!**

End of the day:

How did I feel when I spoke to that colleague or friend? How did they
respond?

_____

_____

_____

_____

Name five kind people I have in my life right now. What gets them on
this list?

_____

_____

_____

_____

Be kind, for everyone you meet is fighting a hard battle.
Plato

https://www.facebook.com/groups/preventingteacherburnout

Friday

Date:_____

First thing:

This week, have I seen moments of mental fitness? When? Has this helped my week?

_____

_____

_____

Today I commit to leaving a note for a colleague, smiling at someone who isn't doing well and complimenting another person. Yes or no?

_____

_____

_____

Tip: As we give out to others, we receive back so much more, even when we are exhausted.

End of the day:

What happened when I showed kindness to others? What was the impact on them and also on me?

_____

_____

_____

_____

What was my best moment today? Why was it so good?

_____

_____

_____

_____

Nourishing yourself in a way that helps you blossom in the direction
you want to go is attainable, and you are worth the effort.
Deborah Day

Weekend

Date:_____

First thing:

My goal this past week for mental fitness - what worked and what didn't?

_____

_____

_____

What did I do this week that had the greatest impact on me?

_____

_____

_____

What did I do this week that had the greatest impact on others?

_____

_____

_____

Tip: A goal keeps us focused and more productive!

End of the day:

What goal can I set for myself for the coming week?

_____

_____

_____

_____

Goals are like magnets. They'll attract the things that make them come true.
Tony Robbins

WEEK - 5
ARE BOUNDARIES REALLY NECESSARY?

Monday

Date:_____

First thing (or Sunday evening):

This week I will look at my boundaries - how do I use my time, energy and resources. These are all limited, so which ones are my greatest concern?

e.g. are my relationships healthy, am I able to address my priorities, am I constantly distracted, do I use my time wisely, am I overcommitted with things I don't believe in….?

_____

_____

_____

_____

Right now, to start my week, what is one boundary I can set?

_____

_____

Tip: Boundaries protect us and empower us; they are not selfish.

End of the day:

Where did I start to notice areas where I have said yes to things that perhaps I shouldn't have, or perhaps I managed to say no to something today? How do I feel about this whole area?

_____

_____

_____

_____

_____

_____

Daring to set boundaries is about having the courage to love ourselves even when we risk disappointing others.
Brené Brown

https://www.facebook.com/groups/preventingteacherburnout

Tuesday

Date:_____

First thing:

Can I identify something that I have said yes to but shouldn't have? Why did I agree at the time?

_____

_____

_____

What action can I take to address this? In taking control, to prioritise myself, however difficult this is, I remind myself today that I matter too. I have value.

_____

_____

_____

Tip: In taking action to put myself first, I may have to take uncomfortable action!

End of the day:

How was my day? Have I taken uncomfortable action? Do I need to ask a trusted person for help to plan to do this? How am I feeling? How can I become hopeful with even a small, planned step?

_____

_____

_____

_____

Two amazing things that happened today:

_____

_____

_____

_____

When you say yes to others, make sure you are not saying no to yourself.
Paulo Coelho

https://www.facebook.com/groups/preventingteacherburnout

Wednesday

Date:_____

First thing:

What are my priorities for today? Choose two that are important to me:

_____

_____

_____

_____

How can I make them happen? Can I schedule them in? Can I ask for help? Do I need resources? Should I plan something in order to enable these?

_____

_____

_____

Tip: Book your priorities into your calendar- then they happen!

End of the day:

Did I achieve my priorities? Even a small step forward counts as a win! How does this make me feel? If I didn't, tomorrow is another day!

_____

_____

_____

_____

After school today, did I use my time wisely? Was it effective? Why? Name one thing that was helpful:

_____

_____

_____

_____

Time is what we want most, but what we use worst.
William Penn

https://www.facebook.com/groups/preventingteacherburnout

Thursday

Date:_____

First thing:

What is going well this week? Is it me or input from others?

_____

_____

_____

That task that is tipping my week - can someone help me with it? Can someone take it off me? Can I talk to someone about it? Who? When? Schedule in to take action:

_____

_____

_____

Tip: Is a task urgent, important or both or neither? Is it your priority today?

End of the day:

Can I see any task that is not a priority or a task that I spend too long on? Can I eliminate it or time block it so it can't take too long? How?

_____

_____

_____

_____

Two encouraging interactions that I had today:

_____

_____

_____

_____

The key to achieving work-life balance is to ruthlessly eliminate
the things that don't matter.
Tim Ferriss

Friday

Date:_____

First thing:

Today I will watch my interactions with my colleagues - when do I say yes to things, and can I say no, or ask for why / clarification. What stops me saying no?

_____

_____

_____

What am I looking forward to today? List three things:

_____

_____

_____

Tip: It's essential to recognise your limits and be comfortable saying no when necessary.

End of the day:

Looking over my week, what have I learnt?

_____

_____

_____

_____

What is one small step I am proud of taking this week to show myself I have worth?

_____

_____

_____

_____

It is better to take many small steps in the right direction than to make a great leap forward only to stumble backward.
Louis Sachar

Weekend

Date:_____

First thing:

What are the five best bits of teaching? Which bits do I love the most?

_____

_____

_____

_____

What are the bits of teaching that I am best at?

_____

_____

_____

Tip: Every day remember that you make a positive impact on many children!

End of the day:

Describe one moment with a child, either this week or previously, that completely made my day:

_____

_____

_____

_____

From my reflections this week, what is one thing I want to do better next week?

_____

_____

_____

_____

The only way to do great work is to love what you do. If you haven't found it yet, keep looking. Don't settle.
Steve Jobs

https://www.facebook.com/groups/preventingteacherburnout

WEEK - 6
AWARENESS: THE KEY TO GROWTH

Monday

Date:_____

First thing (or Sunday evening)**:**

How self-aware do I think I am? Choose a number between 0-100%.
What makes me think this?

_____

_____

_____

_____

This week, can I watch when I become dysregulated? What does this
feel like for me and when does this tend to happen?

_____

_____

_____

Tip: Better self-awareness results in better wellbeing and more confidence.

End of the day:

What even is self-awareness?

_____

_____

_____

_____

What worked today? Where did I show self-awareness? What was the
impact on me or others?

_____

_____

_____

_____

Knowing yourself is the beginning of all wisdom.
Aristotle

Tuesday

Date:_____

First thing:

How do I feel this morning? Can I identify an area in my body where it is holding emotions?

_____

_____

_____

_____

What is one thing I can do today (plan it in), to help me relax and support my own well-being?

_____

_____

_____

Tip: Watch for what works.

End of the day:

What three things worked in my day today?

_____

_____

_____

_____

How does my body feel tonight? Can I describe it? Does it match my mind? Can I take five minutes to simply BE right now and celebrate the wins from my day?

_____

_____

_____

_____

Self-awareness is the key to self-mastery.
Gretchen Rubin

Wednesday

Date:_____

First thing:

How do I feel this morning? What emotions are buzzing round my head?
If there is something I feel I CAN'T do, how can I change it to I CAN?
e.g. with help?

_____

_____

_____

Can I agree in difficult situations to ask WHAT can I do about it, rather
than WHY did it go wrong? How do I feel about this?

_____

_____

_____

Tip: Ask WHAT could I have done better, not WHY didn't it work!

End of the day:

What was a situation that didn't go as I wanted? How did I react?

_____

_____

_____

_____

How am I feeling about my day? Can I identify the positives and focus
on two situations where I'm pleased with my reactions?

_____

_____

_____

_____

Self-awareness gives you the capacity to learn from your mistakes as well as
your successes. It enables you to keep growing.
Lawrence Bossidy

https://www.facebook.com/groups/preventingteacherburnout

Thursday

Date:_____

First thing:

Can I write down the main things I am juggling today, both at home and school?

_____

_____

_____

_____

If I feel overloaded in an area, how would it feel to be vulnerable at school with someone? Is it worth the risk? Who might I ask?

_____

_____

_____

Tip: Vulnerability = courage = strength!

End of the day:

Have I found a small solution to one problem area I am currently contending with? Even a small step is positive. How do I feel about it?

_____

_____

_____

_____

Can I tell myself what a good job I did with a tricky situation today, as if I was getting a response from a trusted colleague? Describe why it succeeded:

_____

_____

_____

_____

If we are brave enough, often enough, we will fall. These are the physics of vulnerability.
Brené Brown

https://www.facebook.com/groups/preventingteacherburnout

Friday

Date:_____

First thing:

How self-aware am I? Can I ask three colleagues today if they think they are self-aware? (The statistics are revealed tomorrow!) Who will I ask?

_____

_____

_____

If self-awareness is "conscious knowledge of one's own character and feelings" (Oxford Learner's dictionary), which of my colleagues do I consider self-aware?

_____

_____

_____

Tip: Your own reactions to situations are your own responsibility.

End of the day:

Do my colleagues think they are self-aware? Do I think they are?

_____

_____

_____

_____

What is a situation today where I could have reacted differently? Might it have changed the outcome?

_____

_____

_____

_____

Self-awareness is one of the rarest of human commodities. I don't mean self-consciousness where you're limiting and evaluating yourself. I mean being aware of your own patterns.
Tony Robbins

https://www.facebook.com/groups/preventingteacherburnout

Weekend

Date:_____

First thing:

How do I feel about my week? Which three children or adults responded positively to what I contributed. Why?

_____

_____

_____

_____

If I am feeling overwhelmed, how can I break down one situation that is on my mind into small steps so I can find a way through it?

_____

_____

_____

Tip: 95% of us think we are self-aware. Reality is 10-15% actually are! Are you?

End of the day:

As I become more self-aware, do I seem to be increasingly regulated?

_____

_____

_____

_____

What are five things or people I am grateful for in my home life at the moment?

_____

_____

_____

_____

The more you know yourself, the more patience you have for
what you see in others.
Erik Erikson

WEEK - 7

WHAT IS THE 5:1 JUGGLE?

Monday

Date:_____

First thing:

If I could take one practical, actionable step this week, what would it be? Why?

_____

_____

_____

Who in my life supports and inspires me to be my best self? In what ways do they do this? Can I check in with them today?

_____

_____

_____

Tip: We need 5:1 positive to negative interactions in our day to stay healthy (Maureen Gaffney).

End of the day:

Name two positive and one negative interaction today. What went well and what went wrong?

_____

_____

_____

_____

What is a situation today where I could have reacted differently? Might it have changed the outcome?

_____

_____

_____

_____

Positive interactions create a ripple effect of goodness. Your small acts of kindness and compassion can have a profound impact on the world around you.
Brendon Burchard

Buy My Book Here: www.rowenahicks.com/books
(More information is in Chapter 4)

Tuesday

Date:_____

First thing:

Happy Tuesday to me! What two people on my team need kindness today? Do I know why?

_____

_____

_____

Can I agree to try to offer three positive interactions during my day? What might these look like?

_____

_____

_____

Tip: Remember, if we have fewer than 3:1 positive to negative interactions, we lose energy and enthusiasm.

End of the day:

Did I achieve positive interactions? How many can I remember? How do I feel and how did the others respond?

_____

_____

_____

_____

I am so glad today that…..

_____

_____

_____

_____

Every interaction is an opportunity to make a positive impact on someone's life. Choose to be the person who lifts others up.
Brendon Burchard

https://www.facebook.com/groups/preventingteacherburnout

Wednesday

Rowena Hicks

Date:_____

First thing:

What are the five main things I am juggling this week?

_____

_____

_____

_____

What are the five main things I have achieved so far this week?

_____

_____

_____

Tip: Focus on a positive….and again…..and again…

End of the day:

Did I take note of interactions more today? Can I note 5:1 positive to negative?

_____

_____

_____

_____

How is my body feeling right now? Do I need to relax my face? My neck? Maybe to take a few breaths? What helps as I slow down?

_____

_____

_____

_____

Positive interactions with others can be the fuel that ignites
your motivation, inspiration, and overall success.
Brendon Burchard

https://www.facebook.com/groups/preventingteacherburnout

Thursday

Date:_____

First thing:

What is one strength I have that I am confident about? Why?

_____

_____

_____

_____

Am I a drain or a radiator? Do I bring positivity to those around me or the opposite? What evidence do I have for this?

_____

_____

_____

Tip: Negative situations will overwhelm us if we don't notice and remember the positives.

End of the day:

Describe a positive interaction I had today. How was the other person's body language?

_____

_____

_____

_____

What situation do I have that is making me feel negative, or overwhelming me? What is one step I can take tomorrow to reduce this stress?

_____

_____

_____

_____

The quality of your life is directly proportional to the
quality of your relationships.
Brendon Burchard

Friday

Date:_____

First thing:

What has been the highlight of my week? Why?

_____

_____

_____

_____

How would I describe my relationships with two people I work closely with? What are the two most positive things about these relationships?

_____

_____

_____

Tip: Remember we need 5:1 positive to negative interactions.

End of the day:

How do I feel about my ratio right now? Where do my positives mainly come from?

_____

_____

_____

_____

In what ways have I fostered positive interactions with people in my life today? How does this make me feel? Am I proud, frustrated, amazed, angry, or relieved?

_____

_____

_____

_____

*In every encounter and every interaction, we must leave the world
a better place than we found it.
Rod Marchand*

https://www.facebook.com/groups/preventingteacherburnout

Weekend

Date:_____

First thing:

What do I commit to doing today for myself? It might feel selfish, but it is the best self-care:

_____

_____

_____

_____

Am I taking enough care of myself? Food? Exercise? Friends and family? Time just for me? Time not thinking about work?

_____

_____

_____

Tip: Small steps make a huge impact!

End of the day:

How did I do with switching off and taking care of myself today?

_____

_____

_____

_____

What is one relationship that is really feeding me right now? How do I support the other person? Is there something I can do to grow this?

_____

_____

_____

_____

The power to change your life lies in the simplest of steps.
Mel Robbins

WEEK - 8
SELF-CARE STRATEGY WEEK

Monday

Date:_____

First thing:

How do I define a self-care focus week? Dare I ask colleagues what they would put into a self-care week?

_____

_____

_____

Could I set a target this week with a safe colleague for one new habit I will put in place to prioritise myself? What? Who can I ask?

_____

_____

_____

Tip: What works for you may not work for someone else.

End of the day:

Have I started my new habit? What are the barriers? What have I achieved?

_____

_____

_____

_____

My physical, mental and emotional well-being are all equally important. What can I do this week to take courageous action for myself?

_____

_____

_____

_____

Self-care is not a one-size-fits-all approach. Discover what works best for you and make it a non-negotiable part of your routine.
Jim Kwik

https://www.facebook.com/groups/preventingteacherburnout

60

Tuesday

Date:_____

First thing:

When in my day and week do I feel my best? Who gets the best of me? Why?

_____

_____

_____

_____

Do the right people get the best of me? What's ONE thing I can do today to re-balance this? How do I take a small step towards righting it, if it's off balance?

_____

_____

_____

Tip: Energy comes from seeing the impact we have in the lives of others.

End of the day:

How is my confidence right now? What are two areas I feel confident in? Why?

_____

_____

_____

_____

Can I commit this week to taking my emails off my phone or stopping work an hour earlier than usual? What might be the impact?

_____

_____

_____

_____

It's not the daily increase but daily decrease. Hack away at the inessentials.
Bruce Lee

https://www.facebook.com/groups/preventingteacherburnout

Wednesday

Date:_____

First thing:

Have I managed to repeat my new habit? e.g. I am taking a lunch break, leaving on time once a week, increasing my exercise, watching my self-talk….

_____

_____

_____

What is going better than I thought this week? Why is that?

_____

_____

_____

Tip: We need to look after mind, body and soul.

End of the day:

Have I done one thing today to remind myself that I matter too? What?

_____

_____

_____

_____

Who have I had a meaningful chat with so far this week? What made it a worthwhile conversation? Can I look to have another?

_____

_____

_____

_____

Self-care is not selfish; it's self-preservation. Prioritising your well-being allows you to show up as your best self and make a greater impact in the world.
Jim Kwik

https://www.facebook.com/groups/preventingteacherburnout

Thursday

Date:_____

First thing:

What can I congratulate myself for overcoming so far this week?

_____

_____

_____

If someone had been watching me all week, what five things would they have praised me for?

_____

_____

_____

Tip: Internal validation is so much more powerful than external validation.

End of the day:

Is there a moment today when I thought I would become dysregulated? What happened? How did I manage? What can I do better next time?

_____

_____

_____

_____

What did I do today to remind myself that I care about ME? One small thing? If I haven't done it yet - can I do something now? Even five minutes of peace can help:

_____

_____

_____

_____

Seeking validation from others is a never-ending cycle. Break free by recognising your own inherent value and finding validation from within.
Peter Sage

https://www.facebook.com/groups/preventingteacherburnout

Friday

Date:_____

First thing:

What has been the highlight of my week? Why?

_____
_____
_____
_____

How would I describe my relationships with two people I work closely with? What are the two most positive things about these relationships?

_____
_____
_____

Tip: Create moments of balance in my life to thrive.

End of the day:

How do the mix of responsibilities alongside my passions balance at the moment?

_____
_____
_____
_____

What activities do I engage in currently that bring me joy?

_____
_____
_____
_____

Reminder: Self-care shouldn't be a reward for when you get all your work done.
Summer Telban

Weekend

Date:_____

First thing:

What are my summary thoughts about my self-care week? What has changed?

_____

_____

_____

This weekend, I agree to doing the following for myself:

_____

_____

_____

Tip: Self-care requires proactive steps!

End of the day:

What has bought me joy this week? Why?

_____

_____

_____

_____

In my current situation, what would a good friend be saying to me right now about how I look after myself?

_____

_____

_____

_____

Self-compassion allows us to embrace our imperfections and treat ourselves with kindness and understanding.
Unknown

https://www.facebook.com/groups/preventingteacherburnout

WEEK - 9
WHAT'S MY CONTRIBUTION?

Monday

Date:_____

First thing:

What is one goal I have for this week? Perhaps that task I've been putting off?

_____

_____

_____

_____

What am I going to do today to remind myself that I matter too?

_____

_____

_____

Tip: Watching for your impact is a key to understanding your value!

End of the day:

Did I achieve my goal today? If not, what small step can I take to start to make it a reality tomorrow?

_____

_____

_____

_____

What three people come to my mind who I have positively impacted today? How?

_____

_____

_____

_____

Being deeply seen, heard, and understood is an essential need of the human heart.
Brené Brown

https://www.facebook.com/groups/preventingteacherburnout

Tuesday

Date:_____

First thing:

Do I believe in myself? What does this even mean?

_____

_____

_____

_____

Today I commit to jotting down each time I have a WIN in my day.

_____

_____

_____

_____

Tip: By noticing our WINS (where we made a significant impact), we start to thrive.

End of the day:

What were my WINS, and how do I feel about them now?

_____

_____

_____

_____

Do I tend to notice my WINS? How can I start to watch for them more?

_____

_____

_____

_____

The value of a man resides in what he gives and not in what he
is capable of receiving.
Albert Einstein

Wednesday

Date:_____

First thing:

Did I take note of Albert Einstein's quote yesterday? Do I agree with it? Why?

_____

_____

_____

_____

What do I give each day that has value?

_____

_____

_____

_____

 Tip: Today I will notice the impact I have on others!

End of the day:

How did I feel today when I contributed to someone over and above?

_____

_____

_____

_____

Note the quote below. It's the same as yesterday! Can I list three ways I "gave out" today that no one else noticed?

_____

_____

_____

_____

The value of a man resides in what he gives and not in what he is capable of receiving.
Albert Einstein

Thursday

Date:_____

First thing:

What are three things I love most about teaching?

_____

_____

_____

_____

As I take a moment now, even in the rush of the start of the day, take five minutes to breathe. Notice how my body feels. Relax my muscles - face, shoulders, tongue, toes, everywhere!

_____

_____

_____

Tip: Slow down! Even making the difference to one person today makes the day worth it. A smile? A kind word? Make them a coffee?

End of the day:

Who did I impact today? How did I help and what difference did I make?

_____

_____

_____

_____

Five things that are going well in my life right now! Five good things! Celebrate these!

_____

_____

_____

_____

The best way to find yourself is to lose yourself in the service of others.
Mahatma Gandhi

https://www.facebook.com/groups/preventingteacherburnout

Friday

Date:_____

First thing:

What am I worrying about this morning?

_____

_____

_____

_____

What is one action I can take to reduce the worry in one area of my life?

_____

_____

_____

_____

Tip: Small steps, one at a time, make a big difference.

End of the day:

Can I write the key components of my self-talk right now? Is it negative?

_____

_____

_____

_____

How can I re-frame some of my self-doubt to remind myself of my skills and impact?

_____

_____

_____

_____

The journey of a thousand miles begins with a single step.
Lao Tzu

Weekend

Date:_____

First thing:

When did my week go better than I thought it would?

_____

_____

_____

_____

What am I frustrated about this week? Perhaps my reaction, someone's response to me, something that didn't work, other?

_____

_____

_____

_____

Tip: When we make mistakes, and we all do, we learn and try again!

End of the day:

What am I looking forward to most this weekend?

_____

_____

_____

_____

How do I feel about Yoda's quote below? Do I agree? Do I see failure in this way?

_____

_____

_____

_____

The greatest teacher, failure is.
Yoda

https://www.facebook.com/groups/preventingteacherburnout

WEEK - 10

WHAT ABOUT ME?

Monday

Date:_____

First thing:

What am I looking forward to this week? If I'm not sure, how can I infuse creativity into my week?

_____

_____

_____

What am I going to do today to remind myself that I matter too?

_____

_____

_____

Tip: Remember- you can't give from an empty pot!

End of the day:

On a scale of 1-10, how "full or empty" do I feel? Do I feel drained, have some sparks of hope and energy, or am I brimming with motivation and creativity?

_____

_____

_____

_____

What can I agree with myself to do, at the start this week, to fill up my own energy tank?

_____

_____

_____

_____

Education is not the filling of a pail, but the lighting of a fire.
William Butler Yeats

https://www.facebook.com/groups/preventingteacherburnout

Tuesday

Date:_____

First thing:

What five words best describe how I feel this morning?

_____

_____

_____

_____

What five things am I grateful for today? Health? Friends? Plans?....

_____

_____

_____

_____

Tip: A moment of gratitude can tip your day in another direction!

End of the day:

What is one thing that went really well today? Why?

_____

_____

_____

_____

What part of my day that goes really well, that I've got nailed, have I stopped noticing and being grateful for?

_____

_____

_____

_____

Gratitude can transform common days into thanksgivings, turn routine jobs into joy, and change ordinary opportunities into blessings.
William Arthur Ward

https://www.facebook.com/groups/preventingteacherburnout

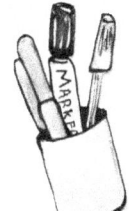

Wednesday

Date:_____

First thing:

Today I choose to look forward to making a difference to the children I work with. What are the names of two children I can focus on who need a boost?

_____

_____

_____

What about me? What do I need today? One thing I can do to support myself?

_____

_____

_____

Tip: Positive affirmations are powerful!

End of the day:

How is my energy right now? What one thing added to my energy stores today? Even a fleeting moment?

_____

_____

_____

_____

How can I celebrate the impact I had on others today? Can I focus on the difference I made?

_____

_____

_____

_____

We rise by lifting others.
Robert Ingersoll

https://www.facebook.com/groups/preventingteacherburnout

Thursday

Date:_____

First thing:

What job will I complete today that I've been trying to avoid? How can I make it happen?

_____

_____

_____

Stop and notice my body for a moment. Is my breathing fast or slow? Are my facial muscles relaxed? Are my shoulders hunched? Can I make adjustments?

_____

_____

_____

Tip: Our body and mind are inextricably entwined.

End of the day:

Did I get that one job done today? How do I feel? If not, try tomorrow?

_____

_____

_____

_____

How can I help myself relax before I sleep? Leave my phone? Listen to music? What helps?

_____

_____

_____

_____

Your body hears everything your mind says. Stay positive.
Unknown

Friday

Date:_____

First thing:

Today I commit to standing up straighter, shoulders back, smiling and watching my breathing. Tonight, I will log the impact.

_____

_____

_____

_____

What am I going to do today to remind myself that I matter too?

_____

_____

_____

Tip: Confuse your brain with a new body signal to contradict your feelings.

End of the day:

What happened as I changed my body signals? Did I notice any changes?

_____

_____

_____

_____

What are three good moments from my week?

_____

_____

_____

_____

The mind and body are not separate entities. They are intimately connected, and each affects the other.
Tony Robbins

https://www.facebook.com/groups/preventingteacherburnout

Date:_____

First thing:

How is my self-talk this morning? Check out the quote below. Do I agree? What can I do today to improve my self-talk?

_____

_____

_____

What am I going to do today to get myself moving in a manner that improves my wellbeing, my health and my mind?

_____

_____

_____

_____

Tip: Investing in yourself reminds your mind that you have value.

End of the day:

How are my energy levels today? How do they compare to Monday?

_____

_____

_____

_____

What three things have made a difference to my week? Did I find things to fill up my energy tank? What can I try for next week?

_____

_____

_____

_____

Your body is the direct result of how you talk to yourself, how
you move, and how you fuel yourself.
Tony Robbins

https://www.facebook.com/groups/preventingteacherburnout

WEEK - 11

TRANSFORMATIVE SELF-TALK

Monday

Date:_____

First thing:

How is my self-talk this morning? Check out the quote below. Do I agree? What can I do today to improve my self-talk?

_____

_____

_____

What am I going to do today to get myself moving in a manner that improves my wellbeing, my health and my mind?

_____

_____

_____

Tip: Investing in yourself reminds your mind that you have value.

End of the day:

How are my energy levels today? How do they compare to last week?

_____

_____

_____

What three things make a difference to my energy tank? Have I got a plan to ensure they are part of my week?

_____

_____

_____

_____

The body says what words cannot.
Bessel van der Kolk

https://www.facebook.com/groups/preventingteacherburnout

Tuesday

Date:_____

First thing:

What is one thing that went well yesterday?

_____

_____

_____

_____

What is one thing to complete so that at the end of the day I can congratulate myself that I DID IT?

_____

_____

_____

Tip: Choose that task you have been putting off and see how it feels to actually get rid of it!

End of the day:

Did I manage to complete that task (I'd been putting off)? Did I take a step towards completing it? How does that feel?

_____

_____

_____

_____

What am I grateful for from today?

1_____

2_____

3_____

Our value doesn't come from our success or our material possessions. It comes from our character, our actions and the positive impact we have on others and the world around us.
Anon

Wednesday

Date:_____

First thing:

How does my body feel this morning? Can I take a moment to focus on letting my shoulders fall, jaw relax, forehead relax? Does this help?

_____

_____

_____

What is a negative self-talk I tell myself? Can I re-phrase it this morning to turn it into a positive? e.g. I can't do it….I'm going to do my best today.

_____

_____

_____

Tip: Reframing negative thoughts takes practice, but it can change your entire outlook.

End of the day:

What has gone well in my day today? Am I relieved? Proud? Excited? Energised?

_____

_____

_____

_____

Have I treated myself with kindness today, both in actions and thoughts? If so, how? If not enough, how can I plan to improve tomorrow?

_____

_____

_____

_____

Talk to yourself as you would someone you love.
Brene Brown

https://www.facebook.com/groups/preventingteacherburnout

CH, FLOURISH,
THRIVE

Thursday

Date:_____

First thing:

Imagine your best self. Describe how you talk to yourself in that state:

_____
_____
_____
_____

What can I do today to start talking to myself like my best self would?

_____
_____
_____

Tip: Visualising your best self can help you align your current behaviour and self-talk with your goals and values.

End of the day:

Where did I succeed today? Even small things? How does that feel?

_____
_____
_____
_____

Can I go to sleep tonight remembering five people I'm grateful for in my life, and being thankful for them? Who are my top five today?

_____
_____
_____
_____

Change your thoughts thurd you change your world.
Norman Vincent Peale

Friday

Date:_____

First thing:

How is my energy today? What is one thing I can plan to do today that I know creates energy for me?

_____

_____

_____

Reflect on this week's journaling. What changes have I noticed? How will I continue to practice positive self-talk?

_____

_____

_____

Tip: Your inner conversations are like seeds you sow and one day, they will grow into the plants you live amongst.

End of the day:

Speak to yourself with the same kindness, praise, and encouragement you would provide to your best friend. So, what do you say to yourself tonight?

_____

_____

_____

And some more?

_____

_____

_____

_____

The words you speak become the house you live in.
Hafiz

https://www.facebook.com/groups/preventingteacherburnout

Weekend

Date:_____

First thing:

Write about one thing I've done this week to improve my self-talk and why I'm proud of that effort.

_____

_____

_____

What was my biggest win this week?

_____

_____

_____

_____

Tip: Improving our self-talk is a marathon not a sprint. Celebrate small wins.

End of the day:

How can I turn a negative thought I had today into a positive?

_____

_____

_____

_____

How are my energy levels today? How do they compare to Monday?

_____

_____

_____

_____

According to the National Science Foundation, it is estimated that the average person has about 12,000 to 60,000 thoughts per day. Of those, 80% are negative and 95% are repetitive thoughts from the day before.

https://www.facebook.com/groups/preventingteacherburnout

WEEK - 12

KINDNESS TO YOURSELF AND OTHERS

Monday

Date:_____

First thing:

What are three things that I know are my strengths? Both at work and also at home?

_____

_____

_____

_____

What are three areas where I feel inadequate or not good enough, that I can challenge myself to improve this week?

_____

_____

_____

Tip: Take time today to listen to yourself talk, to build an awareness of which areas you don't feel good enough in.

End of the day:

List some of the negative self-talk that I have noted through the day:

_____

_____

_____

_____

What positive things can I tell myself when I recognise that negative self-talk starting?

_____

_____

_____

_____

You are allowed to be both a masterpiece and a work in progress
simultaneously.
Sophia Bush

https://www.facebook.com/groups/preventingteacherburnout

Tuesday

Date:_____

First thing:

Who do I know at work who is feeling worried about something, and how could I encourage them in that situation?

_____

_____

_____

_____

Identify two colleagues I work closely with and share their strengths with them. Observe the impact this has on them. Who?

_____

_____

_____

Tip: Reflect on the impact on YOU as you highlight the strength in OTHERS!

End of the day:

What was the impact of building up others on them?

_____

_____

_____

_____

Consider the way I encouraged others today and reflect on the words used and whether I can use them on myself. How does this feel?

_____

_____

_____

_____

The greatest gift you can give someone is your time, your attention, your love, and your concern.
Joel Osteen

Wednesday

Date:_____

First thing:

What are two things that have gone well so far this week? Small or big!

_____

_____

_____

_____

What challenge am I facing today? How can I approach it in a way that I would tell my best friend to?

_____

_____

_____

Tip: Show yourself the same kindness and encouragement that you would show a friend.

End of the day:

How did I manage any challenges I faced today?

_____

_____

_____

_____

Did I show any kindness and encouragement to myself today? How did it influence the outcome of situations?

_____

_____

_____

_____

The smallest act of kindness is worth more than the grandest intention.
Oscar Wilde

Thursday

Date:_____

First thing:

Is there one safe person who I can talk to about an area I feel inadequate in? Who is it, what is the issue, and can I talk to them today?

_____

_____

_____

_____

Name one child who needs me to be their safe person today:

_____

_____

_____

_____

Tip: Being vulnerable enables us to connect in a deeper way with others.

End of the day:

Was I able to be vulnerable? What happened?

_____

_____

_____

_____

How do I feel tonight? Was it a good day? Why?

_____

_____

_____

_____

*Self-compassion is simply giving the same kindness to ourselves that
we would give to others.*
Christopher Germer

https://www.facebook.com/groups/preventingteacherburnout

Friday

Date:_____

First thing:

What is one way in which I can show myself kindness in my busy Friday today?

_____

_____

_____

Thinking about my day - where in my day today can I use my greatest and most valued strength? What is it and when?

_____

_____

_____

Tip: Take sixty seconds, three times, to take deep slow breaths today!

End of the day:

Did I manage to show myself kindness in the busyness? How did it go and how did it feel?

_____

_____

_____

_____

What did I notice in my body during the sixty seconds of deep, slow breaths. If I haven't tried it yet - try now! How does it feel?

_____

_____

_____

_____

The Sleep Foundation shared findings indicating that mindful breathing exercises before bed led to a 30% improvement in sleep quality and a reduction in insomnia symptoms by 25%.

Weekend

Date:_____

First thing:

What can I plan into my day that will bring me some joy? Something that I feel competent in?

_____

_____

_____

_____

Who can I connect with this weekend, who also brings me joy and builds me up?

_____

_____

_____

Tip: Building relationships with friends and family is a worthy investment!

End of the day:

Did I manage to prioritise myself at all today? How do I feel about it?

_____

_____

_____

_____

Can I identify any negative feelings about how I felt about putting myself first? What can I tell myself to challenge those feelings?

_____

_____

_____

_____

Self-care is giving the world the best of you, instead of what's left of you.
Katie Reed

https://www.facebook.com/groups/preventingteacherburnout

WEEK - 13
DO VULNERABILITY AND HUMILITY FEEL LIKE A GOOD IDEA?

Monday

Date:_____

First thing:

Who are the safe adults in my life right now? What makes them safe for me?

_____

_____

_____

_____

Can I remember a time I was vulnerable and how it positively impacted me or someone else?

_____

_____

_____

Tip: According to a study by Dr. Brené Brown, embracing vulnerability can lead to stronger relationships both at home and work.

End of the day:

What is one thing I do have control over at the moment and one thing I don't. Is this OK?

_____

_____

_____

_____

What was a win I had today that surprised me?

_____

_____

_____

_____

Vulnerability is not winning or losing; it's having the courage to show up and be seen when we have no control over the outcome.
Brené Brown

https://www.facebook.com/groups/preventingteacherburnout

Tuesday

Date:_____

First thing:

How does my body feel this morning? Am I holding stress or anxiety? Can I take a moment to relax these areas? Does this help? Repeat again later?

_____

_____

_____

Can I share a challenge I'm facing with someone I trust, seeing if it opens the door for support and understanding?

_____

_____

_____

Tip: Vulnerability = courage!

End of the day:

Do I show my authentic self at work? If so, to whom? If not, what stops me?

_____

_____

_____

_____

What battles have I had, and overcome, that others don't know about?

_____

_____

_____

_____

The strongest people are not those who show strength in front of us but those who win battles we know nothing about.
Unknown

https://www.facebook.com/groups/preventingteacherburnout

Wednesday

Date:_____

First thing:

Is there something I need to do at the moment that I really don't know how to achieve, or could do with some help? Who dare I ask for help?

_____

_____

_____

Am I open to growth? Am I teachable? Or, in some areas, am I stuck in my ways?

_____

_____

_____

Tip: Self-reflection encourages growth.

End of the day:

When today did I make a decision that really benefitted both me and the other person?

_____

_____

_____

Did I ask for help today? Did I offer to help someone else? How did these go?

_____

_____

_____

_____

Humility is not thinking less of yourself, it's thinking of yourself less.
C.S. Lewis

https://www.facebook.com/groups/preventingteacherburnout

Thursday

Date:_____

First thing:

When have I recently overcome a challenge? How would I describe my actions? Courageous? Inspired? Humble?

_____

_____

_____

Who in my life needs some encouragement today? How can I be the person to lift them a little?

_____

_____

_____

Tip: Humility is concerned with what is right.

End of the day:

How have I reacted recently when I got something wrong? Did I show humility? How might I have responded better?

_____

_____

_____

_____

What have I learnt about myself today that I see as a strength? Have I stepped up, supported others or seen an opportunity to grow?

_____

_____

_____

_____

A superior man is modest in his speech, but exceeds in his actions.
Confucius

https://www.facebook.com/groups/preventingteacherburnout

Friday

Date:_____

First thing:

Who are the people in my life who I see as jewels? Students or adults - what is the quality for each that inspires me?

_____

_____

_____

_____

As I look round me now, can I write down five things that make me smile, have happy memories or that I'm grateful for today?

_____

_____

_____

Tip: Look out for someone else and see the benefits to both.

End of the day:

Did I have time to encourage a child or colleague today? How did it go?

_____

_____

_____

_____

What was my greatest win today? Describe it:

_____

_____

_____

_____

An able and yet humble man is a jewel worth a kingdom.
William Penn

Weekend

Date:_____

First thing:

How was my week? Which part of it am I most proud of?

_____

_____

_____

_____

What am I looking forward to most this weekend?

_____

_____

_____

_____

Tip: Careful planning reduces overload.

End of the day:

Have I seen vulnerability and humility this week? Where?

_____

_____

_____

_____

Do I have a plan for next week to do one thing better? Even a small thing? I know small habits repeated can make a big difference!

_____

_____

_____

_____

Vulnerability sounds like truth and feels like courage. Truth and courage aren't always comfortable, but they're never weakness.
Brené Brown

WEEK - 14
DO YOU KNOW YOUR VALUE?

Monday

Date:_____

First thing:

Can I remember a time when all the work and exhaustion of teaching actually felt like it was worth the effort?

_____

_____

_____

What am I really looking forward to today? Can I list at least two things?

_____

_____

_____

Tip: Start to notice the positive impact you have!

End of the day:

What three wins did I have today where I saw the positive impact I made in the lives of adults or students?

_____

_____

_____

_____

If I stop to recognise for a moment what I bring to the role, can I list at least five things?

_____

_____

_____

_____

You have a profound effect on the lives of the children you support.
Rowena Hicks

https://www.facebook.com/groups/preventingteacherburnout

Tuesday

Date:_____

First thing:

Today, can I keep an eye out for colleagues who I can encourage and validate? Who needs it on my team?

_____

_____

_____

Can I list here three things that I know I am really good at? Does it feel uncomfortable or OK to write these down?

_____

_____

_____

Tip: Keep a daily log of wins. Others may not validate them, but you can!

End of the day:

What were my three greatest achievements that I am proud of today?

_____

_____

_____

_____

How did it feel to watch for others' good practice, wins and achievements? How did they respond to my noticing?

_____

_____

_____

_____

Sometimes I think we go through the school day / week / term at such a fast pace that we don't stop to consider the impact we have.
Rowena Hicks

Buy My Book Here: www.rowenahicks.com/books
(More information is in Chapter 4)

Wednesday

Date:_____

First thing:

Have I planned in some self-care and rest today? Even in the busyness of my day, how can I fit this in?

_____
_____
_____

How do I feel I am doing this week if I don't compare myself to others, but rather I compare myself to yesterday or last week?

_____
_____
_____

Tip: Compare yourself to yesterday, not to someone else.

End of the day:

What small yet meaningful influences did I make today?

_____
_____
_____
_____

What moment today could I describe as thriving? What did this feel like to me and what was I doing?

_____
_____
_____
_____

To love oneself is the beginning of a lifelong romance.
Oscar Wilde

Buy My Book Here: www.rowenahicks.com/books
(More information is in Chapter 4)

Thursday

Date:_____

First thing:

Who or what in my life makes me feel alive at the moment? Can I do or see more of these?

_____

_____

_____

Is something worrying me at the moment that I could share with a colleague? Who? How?

_____

_____

_____

Tip: Ask a colleague how they are, not about their work.

End of the day:

Did I manage to share something with someone today? How did that feel?

_____

_____

_____

_____

Did I have time to ask colleagues how they really were today? How was their body language?

_____

_____

_____

_____

You alone are enough. You have nothing to prove to anybody.
Maya Angelou

Friday

Date:_____

First thing:

When this week have I been the best version of myself? Does this surprise me as I reflect on when and where?

_____

_____

_____

Have I started to notice times when I flourish or flow or thrive? Have I discovered more things that make me thrive?

_____

_____

_____

Tip: Looking after yourself is NOT selfish!

End of the day:

What three things can I congratulate myself for achieving this week?

_____

_____

_____

_____

How have I looked after myself so far this week? Is it enough? What can I put in place for this weekend?

_____

_____

_____

_____

External validation is never a replacement for internal validation. True fulfilment comes from knowing your worth without needing the approval of others.
Peter Sage

Weekend

Date:_____

First thing:

List here the positive impact I have had over this week on the students, parents and colleagues I work with:

_____

_____

_____

What have I learnt this week about myself and my strengths and is there one area I need to work on?

_____

_____

_____

Tip: We learn something new every day. If we can retain this attitude of readiness to learn, we can master new things. Rowena Hicks

End of the day:

Am I starting to understand my worth, my impact, my value? Can I write an affirmation to myself here?

_____

_____

_____

_____

Have I noticed times this week when I flourish, flow or thrive? Can I jot down some examples?

_____

_____

_____

_____

Investment in yourself does not mean you are wrapped up in yourself or self-centred, but it does empower you and those you meet.
Rowena Hicks

https://www.facebook.com/groups/preventingteacherburnout

WEEK - 15

ADAPT TO THRIVE: THE POWER OF TEACHABILITY

Monday

Date:_____

First thing:

As I look this week at how teachable I am, is there one area I know I could really benefit from some input or training with? How do I feel about asking for this today?

_____

_____

_____

Reflect on a time I learned something new in my teaching role. What strengths did I demonstrate?

_____

_____

_____

Tip: Research shows many key benefits from CPD.

End of the day:

Can I think of three new ideas or methods I've been grateful to learn or adopt in my teaching?

_____

_____

_____

_____

How confident do I feel about myself and my skills at the start of this week? What is one area I know I am strong in?

_____

_____

_____

_____

Even small areas where we lack skills, when addressed, can have a huge impact on our wellbeing, energy, effectiveness and outlook.
Rowena Hicks

https://www.facebook.com/groups/preventingteacherburnout

Tuesday

Date:_____

First thing:

What colleague or friend has recently taught me something new? How did this feel to be the student again?

_____

_____

_____

Do I have three friends or colleagues who I could share this week's topic with? Can we agree what we might need to learn together? Am I OK to be vulnerable?

_____

_____

_____

Tip: Recognising our need to be teachable is only for the brave!

End of the day:

What did I overcome today? One area where I thought I couldn't do it, but I did?

_____

_____

_____

_____

How are my energy levels today? What brings me joy that I can add to my planning for the rest of the week? One small thing even?

_____

_____

_____

_____

The capacity to learn is a gift; the ability to learn is a skill; the willingness to learn is a choice.
Brian Herbert

https://www.facebook.com/groups/preventingteacherburnout

Wednesday

Date:_____

First thing:

As I look out of the window this morning, what can I see? Can I describe the skyline? Can I calm my soul as I observe the details?

_____

_____

_____

Think of a time when I successfully adapted to a significant change at school. What did I overcome to make this work?

_____

_____

_____

Tip: Schools are places of constant change and challenge. You manage well!

End of the day:

Can I think of two changes in my teaching career that I am now grateful for?

_____

_____

_____

_____

What are two wins from my day today? Unexpected? Relieved? How do I feel about them?

_____

_____

_____

_____

Anyone who keeps learning stays young.
Henry Ford

Thursday

Date:_____

First thing:

How is my team in school? How do I fit in? Is there one person I'm particularly grateful for?

_____

_____

_____

_____

What feedback have I received recently that can help me grow as a teacher?

_____

_____

_____

Tip: Your team needs you even if they don't say it!

End of the day:

Can I reflect on how I give and respond to feedback? Is this healthy? Helpful?

_____

_____

_____

How does my mind feel tonight? Is it peaceful and calm or busy and frazzled? Can I describe it in four words, then reframe these into a growth sentence?

_____

_____

_____

_____

We all need people who will give us feedback. That's how we improve.
Bill Gates

Friday

Date:_____

First thing:

What is one small thing I am excited about today? It could be a special lunch, an opportunity, a meeting or something completely different:

_____

_____

_____

_____

Can I think of how my ongoing pursuit of knowledge has benefitted my students and colleagues. How have they responded?

_____

_____

_____

Tip: What particular interest do I have in work? Read about it.

End of the day:

How do I respond to Gandhi's quote below? Do I live like that? Could I?

_____

_____

_____

_____

Write a gratitude note to myself about how I've managed my week:

_____

_____

_____

_____

Live as if you were to die tomorrow. Learn as if you were to live forever.
Mahatma Gandhi

https://www.facebook.com/groups/preventingteacherburnout

Weekend

Date:_____

First thing:

Even if I am tired, how does it feel to look forward and make a small plan for myself that I could put into place? What would I LOVE to do?

_____

_____

_____

_____

As I reflect on the past week, have I noticed if I am teachable? What strengths have emerged

_____

_____

_____

Tip: Remember to always be as kind to yourself as you would recommend others are to themselves!

End of the day:

What new skill or area of knowledge would I like to pursue? How can I make this happen?

_____

_____

_____

_____

If I were to give myself two stars and a wish for this week, what have I done well and what could I do better?

_____

_____

_____

_____

The beautiful thing about learning is that nobody can take it away from you.
B.B. King

WEEK - 16
CELEBRATING SMALL STEPS

Monday

Date:_____

First thing:

Are there any tasks in my week that feel "too big" for me today?

_____

_____

_____

How can I break this "too big" task down into smaller, achievable steps?

_____

_____

_____

Tip: Breaking a "too big" task down into smaller steps can reduce overwhelm.

End of the day:

What small steps did I take today to achieve my big task?

_____

_____

_____

_____

How did it feel to achieve that one step?

_____

_____

_____

_____

The secret to getting ahead is getting started. The secret to getting started is breaking your overwhelming tasks into small manageable chunks and then starting on the first one.
Mark Twain

Tuesday

Date:_____

First thing:

What activities am I looking forward to today in the classroom?

_____

_____

_____

Which of my smaller steps am I going to attempt to achieve today?

_____

_____

_____

Tip: Try a timeline for completing each step. This helps prevent procrastination and ensures progress.

End of the day:

Having now competed two of my smaller steps, how am I feeling about the progress of my "big task"?

_____

_____

_____

_____

Do I have others around me who are on this journey of learning? Could I share some of my steps with them? See if they have ideas too?

_____

_____

_____

_____

You may delay, but time will not, and lost time is never found again. Therefore, the sooner you break down your tasks, the sooner you'll find success.
Benjamin Franklin

Wednesday

Date:_____

First thing:

What's one thing that I am grateful for happening this week so far?

_____

_____

_____

_____

Identify how far I have come in overcoming my "big task". How am I feeling?

_____

_____

_____

Tip: "Big tasks" can be overwhelming, give yourself some credit for how you've tackled it so far.

End of the day:

What are the areas of overwhelm in my home life that I can apply this strategy to?

_____

_____

_____

_____

How can I incorporate the breaking down of big tasks in my professional environment and in my personal life?

_____

_____

_____

_____

Our greatest weakness lies in giving up. The most certain way to succeed is always to try just one more time.
Thomas A. Edison

https://www.facebook.com/groups/preventingteacherburnout

Thursday

Date:_____

First thing:

Identify people in my circle whom I can reach out to when I need help:

_____

_____

_____

Small steps may have to be accomplished over days or weeks, that is okay. Is there a small step I can ask someone to assist me with?

_____

_____

_____

Tip: It is okay to ask for help; you do not need to work in isolation.

End of the day:

How did it feel to reach out and ask for help today?

_____

_____

_____

_____

Is there anyone I can reach out to, to help them with their smaller steps?

_____

_____

_____

_____

Talent wins games, but teamwork and intelligence win championships.
Michael Jordan

Friday

Date:_____

First thing:

What wins can I celebrate this week?

_____

_____

_____

_____

How have these wins impacted the atmosphere in the classroom or office?

_____

_____

_____

Tip: It's important to celebrate wins, big and small.

End of the day:

Coming into the weekend, what's one act of kindness I can incorporate into my plans?

_____

_____

_____

_____

How has it felt this week to make gains in what seemed like a "too big" task?

_____

_____

_____

_____

It does not matter how slowly you go as long as you do not stop.
Confucius

Weekend

Date:_____

First thing:

It's important to celebrate the wins I have had during my week. I am worth celebrating! What am I going to do this weekend to celebrate me?

_____

_____

_____

Is there someone I enjoy spending time with that I can include in my celebrations? Make contact and enjoy the time together.

_____

_____

_____

Tip: Just as we shouldn't work in isolation, we also don't have to celebrate in isolation. Community is important.

End of the day:

What is something I am looking forward to this week?

_____

_____

_____

_____

What small steps will I continue with and how can I make them joyful experiences?

_____

_____

_____

_____

The more you praise and celebrate your life, the more there is in life to celebrate.
Oprah Winfrey

WEEK - 17
UNSEEN NO MORE: RECOGNISING YOUR WORTH

Monday

Date:_____

First thing:

We can sometimes feel unseen in work and life. What's one instance I can think of where I've felt lost in the crowd?

_____

_____

_____

Now, describe a time when I have felt seen and supported:

_____

_____

_____

_____

Tip: Remember that your worth is not determined by the recognition of others.

End of the day:

Reflecting on my day, can I describe a time where I felt I helped a colleague or student to feel seen?

_____

_____

_____

_____

Who am I grateful for in my life right now? Can I list three people and say why?

_____

_____

_____

_____

To be seen and to be heard is the aspiration of every human being.
Brené Brown

https://www.facebook.com/groups/preventingteacherburnout

Tuesday

Date:_____

First thing:

Feeling unseen can cause one to be disheartened. How would I encourage someone who is feeling this way today?

_____

_____

_____

With this in mind, how might I talk to myself next time I am feeling unseen?

_____

_____

_____

Tip: Building inner confidence can empower us to navigate situations where we feel unnoticed.

End of the day:

Reflecting on my day, list things that bought me joy:

_____

_____

_____

_____

How am I sleeping at the moment? Am I on a screen right up till bedtime? How do I feel about not looking at my phone for an hour before bed to see if it helps?

_____

_____

_____

_____

Invisibility is the beginning of all suffering.
Fyodor Dostoevsky

Wednesday

Date:_____

First thing:

The negative perceptions we have of ourselves can impact us during times when we are feeling unseen. List some of my strengths that I can identify and then focus on these strengths today during tough moments:

_____

_____

_____

And two more strengths here!

_____

_____

_____

Tip: Feeling unseen is an opportunity to cultivate self-validation.

End of the day:

How did it feel to remind myself of my strengths during challenging moments today?

_____

_____

_____

_____

Was it easy or hard to believe myself?

_____

_____

_____

_____

The moment you doubt whether you can fly, you cease
forever to be able to do it.
J.M. Barrie, Peter Pan

https://www.facebook.com/groups/preventingteacherburnout

Thursday

Date:_____

First thing:

I know it's important to have gratitude days, so today I am going to focus on the positives in my week so far. What's one experience I am grateful for?

_____

_____

_____

How has this positive experience impacted my outlook?

_____

_____

_____

Tip: Focussing on the positives leaves less space for the negative!

End of the day:

With gratitude being my focus this morning, what did I notice about my attitude going into the day?

_____

_____

_____

_____

On reflection, how do I think my attitude impacted how my day went?

_____

_____

_____

_____

The more you practice the art of thankfulness, the more
you have to be thankful for.
Norman Vincent Peale

https://www.facebook.com/groups/preventingteacherburnout

Friday

Date:_____

First thing:

At the end of my week reflecting on feeling unseen, how can I continue to build my positive self-talk to support and validate myself?

_____

_____

_____

List some of the positive statements I will use moving forward:

_____

_____

_____

Tip: When we internalise positive self-talk, it slowly replaces the negative self-talk we've listened to all our lives.

End of the day:

How can I continue to encourage those around me to build their self-confidence, so they are able to manage feeling unseen?

_____

_____

_____

_____

What positive statements can I put up around my classroom to help my students internalise positive self-talk? Or around my office?

_____

_____

_____

_____

You have been criticising yourself for years and it hasn't worked. Try approving of yourself and see what happens.
Louise Hay

Weekend

Date:_____

First thing:

It's the weekend, and it's been a big week of reflection. What's one way I can zone out and have some "quiet mind" time?

_____

_____

_____

Do a little search on the internet and find some ways that most interest me to quiet my mind. Which ones jump out to me? List them below so I have a reference of them for the future:

_____

_____

_____

Tip: One way to quiet your mind is by taking some deep breaths and focusing on where you feel that breath most in your body.

End of the day:

How did I feel when my mind was quiet?

_____

_____

_____

_____

List some things that have happened this weekend that I am grateful for:

_____

_____

_____

_____

Your calm mind is the ultimate weapon against your challenges. So relax.
Bryant McGill

https://www.facebook.com/groups/preventingteacherburnout

WEEK - 18
BUILDING RESILIENCE

Monday

Date:_____

First thing:

Resilience is the ability to bounce back from challenging situations.
What's my understanding of resilience?

_____

_____

_____

_____

What's one situation in which I know I exhibited resilience?

_____

_____

_____

Tip: Resilience is built in a safe environment, not by pushing someone beyond their limits.

End of the day:

What was the atmosphere like in my classroom or workplace today?

_____

_____

_____

_____

How did I support a positive atmosphere or how did I challenge a negative atmosphere?

_____

_____

_____

_____

The greatest glory in living lies not in never falling, but in rising every time we fall.
Nelson Mandela

https://www.facebook.com/groups/preventingteacherburnout

Tuesday

Date:_____

First thing:

As stated in the tip yesterday, resilience is built in a safe environment. It is also built through connection. Who is in my community that I feel safe with and how do they support me?

_____

_____

_____

How can I foster an environment of safety and connection for my students and /or colleagues to build their resilience?

_____

_____

_____

Tip: Looking after your health is an important aspect of being resilient as it helps you to cope under pressure.

End of the day:

What worked well in the workplace today that I am proud of?

_____

_____

_____

_____

It can be hard to wind down at the end of a busy day. What can I do for myself tonight to quieten my mind?

_____

_____

_____

_____

Life doesn't get easier or more forgiving, we get stronger and more resilient.
Steve Maraboli

https://www.facebook.com/groups/preventingteacherburnout

Wednesday

Date:_____

First thing:

Keeping in mind that resilience is our ability to cope with tough things, what's a belief I have about getting through tough things in life?

_____

_____

_____

Who am I grateful for in my life today? How does each of them help me?

_____

_____

_____

Tip: Try speaking to yourself like your best friend would.

End of the day:

Reflecting on my day, what situation bought me pride? Either in myself or someone else:

_____

_____

_____

_____

What's one statement I can focus on for tomorrow to encourage myself? (A list of affirmations is at the end of the book if ideas are needed)

_____

_____

_____

_____

Successful people demonstrate their resilience through their dedication to making progress every day, even if that progress is marginal.
Jonathan Mills

TEACH, FLOURISH, THRIVE

Thursday

Date:_____

First thing:

Encouraging our colleagues and students can change the atmosphere in which we all work, making it a safer environment. List some people I am going to encourage today and make a note of them somewhere to remind myself:

_____

_____

With my growing awareness of self-talk, what statement am I going to focus on today to encourage myself? Alternatively, if I am feeling as though my cup is empty today, what's one thing I can do to take gentle care of myself?

_____

_____

Tip: Encouraging others changes the atmosphere from one of self-doubt to self-belief.

End of the day:

How was I able to encourage others today?

_____

_____

_____

Check in with my body and notice any areas of tension, make a note of them below. Now take a minute or two to do some deep breathing and mind quietening. How am I now?

_____

_____

_____

The joy of encouraging others is that it brightens our own path while lighting the way for theirs.
Dean Graziosi

Friday

Date:_____

First thing:

We have learnt that creating safety is important for resilience-building and part of that is creating a safe space in our mind and challenging our negative self-talk. How do I think I've done this week challenging my negative self-talk?

_____

_____

_____

What are three things I'm really proud of achieving so far this week? Can be big or small:

_____

_____

_____

Tip: Small wins are so important - take notice, they matter!

End of the day:

Reflect on yesterday's body check in and note the areas of tension I'm experiencing now. Are they different from yesterday? What relaxation technique can I use now?

_____

_____

_____

List below three situations that happened this week where I showed I am stronger than I thought:

_____

_____

_____

Celebrate the little things, for they are the foundation upon
which great things are built.
Dean Graziosi

https://www.facebook.com/groups/preventingteacherburnout

Weekend

Date:_____

First thing:

Carving out time to quiet myself on a weekend can be tricky, but how much time can I set aside to do this and what can I to do to get the most out of these precious moments? Maybe I found a technique this week that really worked for me, but if not, can I find and try some others this weekend? What?

_____

_____

Is there someone who recharges my batteries when I spend time with them? Can I reach out to them and organise some time together?

_____

_____

Tip: Remember that batteries recharge more efficiently when they're not being used. Stop, breathe, recharge.

End of the day:

Next time a tough situation arises, or perhaps I'm going through one right now, what am I going to remind myself about resilience?

_____

_____

_____

How am I going to create the safe space to move through the tough time?

_____

_____

_____

Sometimes the most productive thing you can do is relax; it rejuvenates your mind, body, and spirit.
Tony Robbins

WEEK - 19

JUGGLING

Monday

Date:_____

First thing:

This week we're looking at the art of juggling. With so many things to juggle in work and life, the need for our time to be used effectively is important. Have I ever felt that I do so much with very little sense of achievement? What are my thoughts on this?

_____

_____

_____

The quote of the day in mind is an opportunity to reflect on what is important to me in general life. This is a great place to start in working out what my priorities are:

_____

_____

_____

Tip: Studies show that multitasking can reduce productivity by as much as 40%. (American Psychological Association)

End of the day:

What tasks in my schedule today did I find myself looking at and wondering "Is this one of my priorities?"

_____

_____

_____

How many tasks did I do today that I identify as being important to me?

_____

_____

_____

The key is not to prioritise what's on your schedule but to
schedule your priorities.
Stephen Covey

Tuesday

Date:_____

First thing:

A great place to start in establishing some of my priorities is to think about what my goals are both professionally and personally. List three goals each for my professional and personal life:

_____

_____

_____

List some of the priorities that I can focus on scheduling in the coming week:

_____

_____

_____

Tip: Remember that change doesn't occur overnight, be kind to yourself in reorganising your priorities and scheduling.

End of the day:

What's something that bought me joy today that I can be grateful for?

_____

_____

_____

If I was able to create some space for my priorities today, how did that feel? Alternatively, how did I feel looking at my schedule with this new-found awareness?

_____

_____

_____

_____

Great things are not done by impulse, but by a series of small things brought together.
Vincent Van Gogh

Wednesday

Date:_____

First thing:

Not everyone is going to understand or accept my new outlook on priorities. How do I feel about watching what I prioritise, checking it works for me?

_____

_____

_____

Looking at my day, what am I looking forward to most? Why?

_____

_____

_____

Tip: Your time is precious; remember you matter too.

End of the day:

If I was able to schedule my priorities in the workplace today, how did those around me respond to that? Alternatively, how do I think they will respond when I do?

_____

_____

_____

_____

How do I think I can model this behaviour to my students so they can also learn the value of scheduling their priorities?

_____

_____

_____

_____

Time is the most valuable coin in your life. You and you alone will determine how that coin will be spent.
Carl Sandburg

Thursday

Date:_____

First thing:

As I spend time incorporating tasks that have value to me into my schedule, I may see a shift in the way I view the many tasks I ultimately have to do. How do I think making space for my goals will affect my ability to accomplish what I need to?

_____

_____

_____

Write down some positive affirmations to encourage me that I am worth making space in my day for:

_____

_____

_____

Tip: Looking after yourself first will ensure that you remain productive without burnout.

End of the day:

What were some tasks today that lifted my spirits, remembering that they may look small, but that when I draw my focus to them, they will become bigger:

_____

_____

_____

Tonight put aside some time to quiet my mind with the techniques I've been using recently and note any new techniques below. It can take a great deal of mental energy making changes to the way I'm doing life:

_____

_____

_____

Change begins at the end of your comfort zone.
Roy T. Bennett

Friday

Date:_____

First thing:

To start the day, make a list of things that have happened this week which I am grateful for:

_____

_____

_____

_____

What areas of my life are currently demanding the most attention and energy, and how do I feel about the balance between them?

_____

_____

_____

Tip: Gratitude is a powerful tool against overwhelm.

End of the day:

With all the changes in how I juggle my schedule and priorities, how can I ensure these changes are lasting?

_____

_____

_____

What am I going to do tonight to wind down and relax? Remember, deep slow breathing is a great place to start this process. Also, maybe less phone time?

_____

_____

_____

Gratitude bestows reverence, allowing us to encounter everyday epiphanies, those transcendent moments of awe that change forever how we experience life and the world.
John Milton

https://www.facebook.com/groups/preventingteacherburnout

Weekend

Date:_____

First thing:

Have fun this weekend! What have I planned to recharge my batteries and keep these in mind for when I start to feel exhaustion creeping up on me? If I haven't yet got a plan - what do I want to do for ME?

_____

_____

_____

What are the top three priorities in my life right now, and what steps can I take to ensure they receive the focus they need?

_____

_____

_____

Tip: The more you value your time, the more value it will bring.

End of the day:

When did I laugh today? Was it enough? Can I plan for more?

_____

_____

_____

_____

How has my sleep been? Am I looking after my sleep routine? Can I do more? What could I do? Less screen time? Mindfulness? Better routine? Worth it?

_____

_____

_____

Laughter is an instant vacation.
Milton Berle

https://www.facebook.com/groups/preventingteacherburnout

WEEK - 20
OVERCOMING PEOPLE PLEASING

Monday

Date:_____

First thing:

Am I feeling confident about the week ahead? What am I looking forward to?

_____

_____

_____

_____

Reflect on a recent situation where I felt compelled to please someone. What motivated that behaviour?

_____

_____

_____

Tip: You can't please everyone.

End of the day:

How did my day go? Did I set myself up to succeed? What might this look like for tomorrow?

_____

_____

_____

_____

What does it mean for me to be my authentic self?

_____

_____

_____

_____

Studies show that over 60% of people who identify as "people pleasers" often struggle with low self-esteem.

Tuesday

Date:_____

First thing:

Do I have stress around my shoulders, jaw or elsewhere? Can I take a few moments to relax, breathe and focus on something positive? Does this help?

_____

_____

_____

List three boundaries I struggle to maintain. How can respecting these boundaries improve my well-being?

_____

_____

_____

Tip: Setting boundaries is an act of self-respect and self-care.

End of the day:

Did I have any luck putting in a boundary today? When? If not, could I have? What about tomorrow?

_____

_____

_____

_____

Have I shown myself today that I also matter, as well as everyone and everything else? How? If not, how can I tomorrow?

_____

_____

_____

_____

Daring to set boundaries is about having the courage to love ourselves, even when we risk disappointing others.
Brené Brown

https://www.facebook.com/groups/preventingteacherburnout

Wednesday

Date:_____

First thing:

Today I say YES to looking after myself in some new way. What can I change about my day to show myself this?

_____

_____

_____

Can I practice saying "No" in a respectful and firm manner. Use phrases like, "I appreciate the offer, but I can't commit to this right now". Worth a try?

_____

_____

_____

Tip: Your time and energy are valuable, and it's okay to protect them.

End of the day:

Have I been able to protect myself in some small way today? When? How did it feel? If not, what about tomorrow? When might this be possible?

_____

_____

_____

What was my biggest moment of joy today? Why was it so important?

_____

_____

_____

_____

Half of the troubles of this life can be traced to saying yes too quickly and not saying no soon enough.
Josh Billings

146

Thursday

Date:_____

First thing:

How am I feeling today? Honestly? Who is one safe person I can share this with today? Perhaps I can encourage them with my vulnerability?

_____

_____

_____

_____

Can I think of a situation where I was authentically myself. How did it feel compared to people-pleasing?

_____

_____

_____

Tip: Your authentic self is enough; you don't need to please others to be valued.

End of the day:

What is one real and honest moment I had with someone today? How did it go and how did we both feel about it?

_____

_____

_____

_____

How do I feel about putting myself first in situations that perhaps I don't usually? Is this uncomfortable? How have I managed so far this week?

_____

_____

_____

_____

Be yourself; everyone else is already taken.
Oscar Wilde

Friday

Date:_____

First thing:

Which three people am I most grateful to have in my life today? Why?

_____

_____

_____

_____

Reflect on something I'm proud of that doesn't rely on others' approval. How does this internal validation feel?

_____

_____

_____

Tip: Shift your focus from seeking external validation to finding internal satisfaction.

End of the day:

How much do I rely on validation of others to make me feel OK, successful or appreciated? Is this healthy?

_____

_____

_____

_____

It's Friday! What in my week went really well that I'm proud of? Why?

_____

_____

_____

_____

Your value doesn't decrease based on someone's inability to see your worth.
Unknown

https://www.facebook.com/groups/preventingteacherburnout

Weekend

Date:_____

First thing:

What progress have I made this week in overcoming people-pleasing?

_____

_____

_____

_____

Can I plan this weekend for some self-compassion? What might this look like for me to prioritise? What could I do differently to usual?

_____

_____

_____

Tip: You deserve the same compassion and understanding you offer to others.

End of the day:

Have I done something just for myself today? Even something small? How did it feel to do that?

_____

_____

_____

_____

What does it mean to me to be kind to myself? Does it feel selfish? Have I managed this at all this week? How can I grow this?

_____

_____

_____

_____

Talk to yourself like someone you love.
Brené Brown

WEEK - 21
EFFORTLESS ROUTINES, ENDLESS ENERGY

Monday

Date:_____

 (top right: Rowena Hicks logo)

First thing:

What very basic level things can I be thankful for today? Is it a safe bed to sleep in, a pet who keeps me company, energy or food?

_____

_____

_____

What in my morning routine lifts my spirits? If nothing, can I add one small thing? If short of ideas…. try google!

_____

_____

_____

Tip: Simple routines can reduce tiredness.

End of the day:

Am I a routine sort of person? Do I like this idea? How do I feel about watching what my routines look like this week?

_____

_____

_____

_____

What has gone well today? Do I feel proud? Excited? Relieved?

_____

_____

_____

_____

According to a study by the American Psychological Association, 46% of people say that having a consistent morning routine improves their mood and performance.

https://www.facebook.com/groups/preventingteacherburnout

Tuesday

Date:_____

First thing:

What three words best describe how I am feeling this morning? What one small thing can I plan to change one of these words for the better?

_____

_____

_____

How could I better structure my workday to balance teaching, planning and administrative tasks effectively?

_____

_____

_____

Tip: Establish time blocks for different types of work to maintain focus and prevent burnout.

End of the day:

Did I manage to start to time-block my day better? Did it make any difference? What could I try for tomorrow? Can I structure my planning more effectively?

_____

_____

_____

_____

Who am I grateful to have in my life at the moment? Why?

_____

_____

_____

_____

The secret of your future is hidden in your daily routine.
Mike Murdock

https://www.facebook.com/groups/preventingteacherburnout

Wednesday

Date:_____

First thing:

Looking around me this morning, can I list five reasons to be grateful?

_____

_____

_____

_____

How did I sleep last night? How was my evening/sleep routine?

_____

_____

_____

Tip: The National Sleep Foundation reports that having a consistent evening routine improves sleep quality by up to 30%.

End of the day:

What unwinding activities can I include in my evening routine to ensure that I relax and recharge for the next day?

_____

_____

_____

_____

What habits do I currently have to help me relax? Are these good for me?

_____

_____

_____

_____

Finish each day and be done with it. You have done what you could.
Learn from it; tomorrow is a new day.
Ralph Waldo Emerson

https://www.facebook.com/groups/preventingteacherburnout

Thursday

Date:_____

First thing:

What is one positive thing that happened yesterday? Is this unexpected?

_____

_____

_____

_____

How can I create routines that help me manage my work responsibilities while maintaining a fulfilling home life? Do I feel this is possible?

_____

_____

_____

Tip: Separate work and home with a clear boundary.

End of the day:

Did I have enough down-time at home today? Was it quality time with those I love or proper switch-off time? Did work invade home?

_____

_____

_____

_____

Which of my valued strengths did I use today? How did I feel when I used this competency? Can I find a way of using this more?

_____

_____

_____

_____

Balance is not better time management, but better boundary management.
Betsy Jacobson

Friday

Date:_____

First thing:

How can I show kindness to someone today? Who around me needs this?

_____

_____

_____

What small changes can I make to my existing routines to improve my productivity and efficiency?

_____

_____

_____

Tip: Tiny adjustments to your routines can lead to significant improvements in productivity.

End of the day:

Do I feel like my day has been productive? Why? Why not?

_____

_____

_____

_____

What am I proud of achieving this week? Where was I at my best?

_____

_____

_____

_____

Productivity is never an accident. It's always the result of a commitment to excellence, intelligent planning and focused effort.
Paul J. Meyer

https://www.facebook.com/groups/preventingteacherburnout

Weekend

Date:_____

First thing:

As I contemplate my weekend, have I included some self-care space? What does or could this look like for me? Do I believe that I'm worth the effort of prioritising this?

_____

_____

_____

Reflecting on my routines from last week, what works and what could I adjust?

_____

_____

_____

 Tip: Reflect and self-assess for greater productivity.

End of the day:

Did I share a beautiful moment with someone this week? What made it so special?

_____

_____

_____

What am I excited about in the next few days? If nothing, what can I arrange so that I do?

_____

_____

_____

Reflection is one of the most underused yet powerful tools for success.
Richard Carlson

WEEK - 22

DECISION FATIGUE

Monday

Date:_____

First thing:

On a scale of 1-10, how tired do I feel? Can I work out if it's mental or physical tiredness?

_____

_____

_____

Can I take a moment this morning to relax my shoulders, jaw and forehead. Take a few breaths and repeat through the day. Start now - any impact?

_____

_____

_____

Tip: Spend a few minutes each day reflecting on how you feel after making a series of decisions.

End of the day:

Did I notice today when I was making decisions? How do I handle them? For example…

_____

_____

_____

_____

What went well today? Why?

_____

_____

_____

_____

The first step toward change is awareness.
Nathaniel Branden

https://www.facebook.com/groups/preventingteacherburnout

Tuesday

Date:_____

First thing:

Which three people in my life bring me joy right now? How?

_____

_____

_____

_____

What is my biggest decision for today? Can I make it or do I need help?

_____

_____

_____

Tip: Identify the most important decisions you need to make each day and tackle them first when your mind is freshest.

End of the day:

Did I have a patch of my day that went smoothly? What did I do that made it work?

_____

_____

_____

_____

Can I jot down five smaller decisions I got right today?

_____

_____

_____

_____

The key is not to prioritise what's on your schedule but to schedule your priorities.
Stephen Covey

Wednesday

Date:_____

First thing:

How do I feel about trying to simplify just one thing I'm having to do at the moment? What might this be?

_____

_____

_____

If I agree I have very high expectations of myself, what might my friends tell me I could simplify a little today?

_____

_____

_____

Tip: Where possible, simplify your options. For example, streamline or standardise classroom routines to reduce the number of daily decisions.

End of the day:

Have I observed myself making decisions that enable a simpler outcome today? When?

_____

_____

_____

_____

What is one thing that has gone really well today that surprised me? Why?

_____

_____

_____

_____

Simplicity is the ultimate sophistication.
Leonardo da Vinci

TEACH, FLOURISH, THRIVE

Thursday

Date:_____

First thing:

How did I sleep? Do I feel refreshed? Can I try to minimise screen time before bed tonight?

_____

_____

_____

How do I feel about trying to put some boundaries around my decision-making today, so I give myself some time out? Is it even possible?

_____

_____

_____

Tip: Set a specific time aside for making decisions, and once that time is up, move on to other tasks. This helps prevent decision overload.

End of the day:

When did I laugh today?

_____

_____

_____

_____

What is something I achieved today that I am proud of?

_____

_____

_____

_____

Discipline is the bridge between goals and accomplishment.
Jim Rohn

Friday

Date:_____

First thing:

Do I have a good morning routine that is well embedded, or could I improve it?

_____

_____

_____

What has been my biggest weight this week? Biggest challenge. Why?

_____

_____

_____

Tip: Develop daily routines and habits. When certain actions become habitual, they no longer require conscious decision-making, freeing up mental energy.

End of the day:

As I watched my habits and routines, where can I switch off because it's completely habitual?

_____

_____

_____

_____

Who can I send a quick message to right now to celebrate a win this week? What win do I choose?

_____

_____

_____

_____

Motivation is what gets you started. Habit is what keeps you going.
Jim Ryun

Weekend

Date:_____

First thing:

How would I describe my week, and why?

_____

_____

_____

_____

When this week did I have compassion on myself? Can I book in some self-care time this weekend?

_____

_____

_____

Tip: Schedule regular breaks throughout your day, and practice self-care activities such as mindfulness or exercise to rejuvenate your mind and body.

End of the day:

What's one thing that worked this week that I will replicate next week?

_____

_____

_____

_____

What's one thing that didn't work, or made me feel uneasy this week, that I need to avoid next week? How can I do this?

_____

_____

_____

_____

Almost everything will work again if you unplug it for a few
minutes, including you.
Anne Lamott

WEEK - 23
ONE NEW SKILL TO BUILD CONFIDENCE

Monday

Date:_____

First thing:

List three skills I excel at and describe how they contribute to my daily life:

_____

_____

_____

_____

How can I further develop these strengths?

_____

_____

_____

Tip: Focus on what you are already good at and find ways to excel even more. Building on your strengths can boost your confidence significantly.

End of the day:

What did I do today that really worked? Was the impact on me or others?

_____

_____

_____

Where did I use one of my valued strengths today?

_____

_____

_____

_____

Believe in yourself and all that you are. Know that there is something inside you that is greater than any obstacle.
Christian D. Larson

Tuesday

Date:_____

First thing:

What is one thing I'm looking forward to today? Why?

_____

_____

_____

_____

Write down a skill I want to improve. What small, achievable steps can I take this week to start mastering this skill?

_____

_____

_____

Tip: Break larger goals into smaller, manageable tasks to avoid feeling overwhelmed and to create a sense of accomplishment.

End of the day:

Being honest with myself - do I believe I can get better at things?

_____

_____

_____

_____

What might I need to try in order to be or to do better in one of these things?

_____

_____

_____

_____

The future belongs to those who believe in the beauty of their dreams.
Eleanor Roosevelt

https://www.facebook.com/groups/preventingteacherburnout

Wednesday

Date:_____

First thing:

What is one WIN I had yesterday? How did it make me feel? Can I internalise that feeling?

_____

_____

_____

_____

What is one skill I've struggled with? What steps can I take to persist through to overcome this?

_____

_____

_____

Tip: View failure as a learning opportunity rather than a setback.

End of the day:

Do I agree with the quote below? If so, what am I struggling with right now and how can I change my language about how to overcome it?

_____

_____

_____

_____

Write three positive affirmations about myself. How can I remind myself of these through tomorrow?

_____

_____

_____

_____

Success is not final, failure is not fatal: It is the courage to
continue that counts.
Winston Churchill

Thursday

Date:_____

First thing:

What part of today am I looking forward to and why?

_____

_____

_____

_____

Think about a time I've received feedback. How did I react? What can I learn from constructive criticism to enhance my skills?

_____

_____

_____

Tip: Seek feedback from SAFE sources.

End of the day:

How do I honestly feel about feedback? Have I always received / or given constructive feedback?

_____

_____

_____

_____

Do I feel like a champion today? What is my biggest achievement?

_____

_____

_____

_____

Feedback is the breakfast of champions.
Ken Blanchard

TEACH, FLOURISH, THRIVE

Friday

Date:_____

First thing:

How is my week going? What is one thing I can do or say today that can lift it higher? e.g. encourage someone else, finish something I've been putting off…

_____

_____

_____

What new skill would I like to learn? Outline a plan to acquire this skill, including resources and support I might need.

_____

_____

_____

Tip: Continuously seek new skills that interest you and align with your goals.

End of the day:

I made it through the week! What's my biggest victory?

_____

_____

_____

Thinking about developing a new skill - do I agree this is a good idea and can I find the energy to make it happen?

_____

_____

_____

_____

You don't have to be great to start, but you have to start to be great.
Zig Ziglar

Weekend

Date:_____

First thing:

Reflect on my week's progress. What have I learned?

_____

_____

_____

_____

Which daily activities helped my confidence grow the most? How will I continue this growth?

_____

_____

_____

_____

Tip: Recognise your achievements, no matter how small.

End of the day:

Can I celebrate things from my week? Which am I pleased with?

_____

_____

_____

_____

Can I set myself up for next week to grow and achieve again - how?

_____

_____

_____

_____

Celebrate what you want to see more of.
Tom Peters

WEEK - 24

REST IN THE RUSH

Monday

Date:_____

First thing:

Do I feel rested this morning? How is my body and mind? How would I describe them?

_____

_____

_____

_____

Do I know what rest looks like for me? What works?

_____

_____

_____

Tip: Remember, rest isn't a luxury; it's essential for your well-being.

End of the day:

Did I notice times today when I felt most rested or managed to rest? What was I doing?

_____

_____

_____

_____

What was my biggest achievement today? How do I feel about it?

_____

_____

_____

_____

For fast-acting relief, try slowing down.
Lily Tomlin

https://www.facebook.com/groups/preventingteacherburnout

Tuesday

Date:_____

First thing:

Which three people am I most grateful for this morning and why?

_____

_____

_____

_____

How do I feel this morning thinking about rest when my to-do list is so long?

_____

_____

_____

Tip: Remember, we all rest in different ways. Find what works for you!

End of the day:

Did I notice a time of rest today? What was I doing and how did I feel?

_____

_____

_____

_____

Can I list three things I intend to try, book into my diary, to rest better this week? What are they? When can I do them?

_____

_____

_____

_____

Sometimes, the most productive thing you can do is relax.
Mark Black

https://www.facebook.com/groups/preventingteacherburnout

Wednesday

Date:_____

First thing:

What am I looking forward to today? Why?

_____

_____

_____

Write about a moment when I allowed myself guilt-free rest and appreciated it:

_____

_____

_____

Tip: Rest is a right, not a privilege. Give yourself permission.

End of the day:

Do I feel guilty for taking time to rest? Write about those feelings and challenge them:

_____

_____

_____

_____

Is there one thing in my mind that is particularly bothering me at the moment? What? What is one step for tomorrow to take action?

_____

_____

_____

_____

Rest and self-care are so important. When you take time to replenish your spirit, it allows you to serve others from the overflow. You cannot serve from an empty vessel.
Eleanor Brownn

https://www.facebook.com/groups/preventingteacherburnout

Thursday

Date:_____

First thing:

Describe my ideal restful environment. What elements are present? How can I incorporate these elements into my daily life?

_____

_____

_____

_____

Have I discovered yet how I rest best? Is it exercise? A long bath? A chat? What is it that I can make sure I do for myself today?

_____

_____

_____

Tip: Your surroundings can greatly influence your ability to rest. Make small changes to nurture a restful space.

End of the day:

What in my surroundings helps me to rest? Have I noticed it or used it today? Why does this matter?

_____

_____

_____

_____

Do I agree with the quote below? Have I been overlooking rest? What is one, even small, thing I can change right now?

_____

_____

_____

_____

There is virtue in work and there is virtue in rest. Use both and overlook neither.
Alan Cohen

https://www.facebook.com/groups/preventingteacherburnout

Friday

Date:_____

First thing:

Have I noticed how I've been using my time more this week? What have I noticed? Has it helped and brought any small changes?

_____

_____

_____

Try a new, restful activity today. Write about my experience and how it differed from my usual rest routines:

_____

_____

_____

Tip: Be open to trying new restful activities, even those that seem out of your comfort zone.

End of the day:

Did I try something new today to help me rest? How can I rest while at work? Even for two minutes, what could this look like?

_____

_____

_____

_____

What three conversations did I have this week that made me smile or brought me joy?

_____

_____

_____

_____

Sometimes the most important thing in a whole day is the rest we take between two deep breaths.
Etty Hillesum

Weekend

Date:_____

Rowena Hicks

First thing:

I believe in the importance of rest, so why is it so hard for me to include it in my week?

_____

_____

_____

What three lovely things have I booked into my weekend?

_____

_____

_____

Tip: Don't leave rest to chance, it gets squeezed out!

End of the day:

What restful activity can I put into my diary for next week? It can be a small thing like taking twenty seconds before I walk into a room to breathe slowly, or a new sport:

_____

_____

_____

How does my body feel tonight? Tight shoulders? Jaw? How can I take a moment just for me?

_____

_____

_____

_____

Rest when you're weary. Refresh and renew yourself, your body, your mind, your spirit. Then get back to work.
Ralph Marston

https://www.facebook.com/groups/preventingteacherburnout

H, FLOURISH, THRIVE

WEEK - 25

**FUELLING YOUR BEST SELF:
THE POWER OF NUTRITION AND
HYDRATION**

Monday

Rowena Hicks

Date:_____

First thing:

As I look into my eating and drinking habits this week, do I feel good about my habits or where could I improve?

_____

_____

_____

_____

What aspect of this week am I looking forward to most. Why?

_____

_____

_____

Tip: Keep a food and drink diary for a week to identify patterns and areas for improvement

End of the day:

How were my eating and drinking habits today? Is there one area I can improve on tomorrow - how can I make sure this happens?

_____

_____

_____

_____

What self-care activities have helped me unwind after a challenging day? How can I prioritise these moments more often?

_____

_____

_____

_____

The first wealth is health.
Ralph Waldo Emerson

CH, FLOURISH, THRIVE

Tuesday

Date:_____

First thing:

How does my body feel this morning? Tense? Relaxed? Sore? Free?
What can I do to help it out today? One small step.

_____

_____

_____

Did I eat a balanced diet yesterday? Can I rebalance it with a small
change today? Can I then monitor how I feel about this?

_____

_____

_____

Tip: Small changes lead to lasting, healthy habits.

End of the day:

Where did I make a difference to someone today? When? How do I
know? How do I feel about that?

_____

_____

_____

_____

Can I try to stay away from my phone before bed today? How long can I
manage? Am I prepared to see myself as using my phone too much?

_____

_____

_____

_____

According to the CDC (Centres for Disease Control and Prevention), only 1 in
10 adults get enough fruits or vegetables each day.

https://www.facebook.com/groups/preventingteacherburnout

Wednesday

Date:_____

First thing:

How is my water intake? Does a focus on this seem worth it or a time waster?

_____

_____

_____

_____

How is my mood this morning? What can I agree to do for MYSELF today to bring me a boost?

_____

_____

_____

Tip: Staying hydrated boosts your energy and overall well-being.

End of the day:

If staying hydrated boosts my energy and overall well-being, am I doing enough to help myself with this? How can I improve?

_____

_____

_____

_____

Can I list three small wins from today?

_____

_____

_____

_____

The National Academies of Sciences, Engineering, and Medicine recommend daily water intake of about 3.7 litres for men and 2.7 litres for women.

Thursday

Date:_____

First thing:

Looking at today's quote below, do I eat intelligently? Always?
Sometimes? Explain:

_____

_____

_____

_____

What one small step can I take today to eat more healthily? How
important is this to me?

_____

_____

_____

Tip: Eating more healthily gives energy, so it's worth the effort!

End of the day:

What is stopping me eating better? What is helping me to eat more
intelligently?

_____

_____

_____

_____

Who is one person who has shown me kindness today? How did I
respond? How did this make me feel?

_____

_____

_____

_____

To eat is a necessity, but to eat intelligently is an art.
François de La Rochefoucauld

Friday

Date:_____

First thing:

How is my energy this morning? What has drained me this week?

_____

_____

_____

_____

Is there one thing I can put in place today that will boost my energy? Is this food? Is it a break? Is it more water? Is it connecting with a safe friend?

_____

_____

_____

Tip: Working drains energy. Eating well can boost energy. Simple but true!

End of the day:

How do my eating habits change as I get more tired? How have I managed this week?

_____

_____

_____

Can I reach out to a friend to talk about this week's journal? Do I find it inspiring, challenging or just one more thing to think about?

_____

_____

_____

The American Heart Association suggests eating at least five servings of fruits and vegetables per day for optimal health.

Weekend

Date:_____

First thing:

What am I most looking forward to this weekend? Can I make sure I take time for me, to laugh, relax and rest?

_____

_____

_____

What is my main takeaway from thinking about my eating and drinking habits this week? Is it helpful? Can I put in place one new, small habit as a result?

_____

_____

_____

Tip: Meal planning takes time but can reduce cost and improve healthy eating habits.

End of the day:

Can I put a plan in place for next week to make sure I have a balanced diet? Is this easy for me or a mountain of a task? Am I worth the effort?

_____

_____

_____

_____

Looking back at this week, where did I feel "seen"? Who was it, and how did I feel?

_____

_____

_____

_____

Plan your work and work your plan.
Napoleon Hill

WEEK - 26
DISTRACTION DETOX

Monday

Date:_____

First thing:

How does this week ahead look for me? What is likely to be my favourite part? Why?

_____

_____

_____

What are the top three distractions that interfere with my productivity the most? How do they impact my daily life?

_____

_____

_____

Tip: Awareness is the first step towards managing your distractions effectively.

End of the day:

Did I notice how easily (or not) I was distracted today? Is there one thing I could change this week to address this?

_____

_____

_____

_____

Has today been a productive day? When was I most productive? What helped?

_____

_____

_____

_____

According to a study by Udemy, 70% of workers feel distracted while on the job.

https://www.facebook.com/groups/preventingteacherburnout

Tuesday

Date:_____

First thing:

How did I sleep? Was something on my mind? If so, can I write it here with a suggested solution, even a first small step towards finding some peace:

_____

_____

_____

What is the one task I really must complete today? How can I set myself up today to make this happen?

_____

_____

_____

Tip: Use the Eisenhower Matrix to distinguish between urgent and important tasks, focusing primarily on what's both urgent and important.

End of the day:

Did I get distracted today by things? Am I watching for distractions, logging them (even mentally), to see if I can reduce them?

_____

_____

_____

_____

Who or what made my day today? Why was it important for me?

_____

_____

_____

_____

Most of us spend too much time on what is urgent and not enough time on what is important.
Stephen Covey

Wednesday

Date:_____

First thing:

How is my energy this morning? If it's as important to manage my energy as my time, what is one small thing I can do to manage my energy levels?

_____

_____

_____

How do my energy levels fluctuate throughout the day? What can I do to maintain or boost my energy when it dips?

_____

_____

_____

Tip: Even one-minute breaks make a difference to energy.

End of the day:

Did I manage to take some breaks through today? Did I drink enough water? What about healthy eating and some exercise? How am I doing?

_____

_____

_____

_____

Am I feeling like I just can't get enough done? Write here a list of five things I DID achieve today!

_____

_____

_____

_____

Tracking their behaviour, researchers found that breaks can improve productivity by 33%.

https://www.facebook.com/groups/preventingteacherburnout

Thursday

Date:_____

First thing:

What does work life balance mean to me? Does it even exist? If I agree it matters, am I prepared to take action in this area?

_____

_____

_____

How can I create a better balance between my work and personal life? What boundaries do I need to establish?

_____

_____

_____

Tip: Creating balance is a step towards achieving sustainable success.

End of the day:

Did I set a boundary around what time I was going to stop working today? Did it work? What can I try tomorrow?

_____

_____

_____

_____

Can I switch my brain off from work today? What might help me to do this? How about listing three people who are important to me and how I might show them I appreciate them tomorrow?

_____

_____

_____

_____

According to OECD, 66% of employed adults report balancing work and personal life as one of their biggest challenges.

https://www.facebook.com/groups/preventingteacherburnout

Friday

Date:_____

First thing:

When do I multitask? Do I? Can I watch today to see what I really do?

_____

_____

_____

In what ways do I multitask? How can I minimise multitasking to enhance my productivity?

_____

_____

_____

Tip: Research by the American Psychological Association shows that multitasking can reduce productivity by up to 40%.

End of the day:

Did I get distracted by much today? When is it most difficult to focus on tasks I need to complete?

_____

_____

_____

Did I have time for some proper conversations today? Which ones were most valuable to me? Why?

_____

_____

_____

_____

You can do two things at once, but you can't focus effectively
on two things at once.
Gary Keller

Weekend

Date:_____

First thing:

How was this past week? Can I congratulate myself on some WINS I had?

_____

_____

_____

How have my distractions changed over the past week? What strategies can I implement moving forward to manage them better?

_____

_____

_____

Tip: Use apps and tools designed for productivity, such as task managers and focus enhancers, while minimising notifications.

End of the day:

Do I use technology to help me, or is it a big distraction to me? What small step might I take to help myself?

_____

_____

_____

_____

What is my plan for tomorrow to ensure I get rest, refresh, re-energise and take some care of myself?

_____

_____

_____

_____

Without reflection, we go blindly on our way, creating more unintended consequences and failing to achieve anything useful.
Margaret J. Wheatley

https://www.facebook.com/groups/preventingteacherburnout

WEEK - 27

STEADY PULSE: STRATEGIES TO REGULATE EMOTIONS EFFECTIVELY

Monday

Date:_____

First thing:

Which aspects of my life am I grateful for this morning? Can I list three?

_____

_____

_____

_____

What does emotional regulation mean to me, and why is it important in my daily life?

_____

_____

_____

Tip: Understand what situations or experiences typically lead to dysregulation. Awareness is the first step toward managing them.

End of the day:

Has today been a good day for me? Did I notice if, and when, I was well regulated?

_____

_____

_____

_____

How does my body feel tonight? Am I holding stress in my body? Can I take a few minutes to release my shoulders, jaw, eyebrows? Breathe. Better?

_____

_____

_____

_____

You can't control how you feel. But you can always choose how you act.
Mel Robbins

Tuesday

Date:_____

First thing:

What resources or people in my life am I thankful for?

_____

_____

_____

What are the physical and emotional signs that I experience when I am dysregulated?

_____

_____

_____

Tip: Regularly check in with your body and emotions throughout the day to catch early signs of dysregulation.

End of the day:

Did today feel more or less stressful than usual? Why?

_____

_____

_____

_____

Who do I have in my life with whom I can talk through my joys and challenges? What would be my main focus of discussion right now? What might they say?

_____

_____

_____

_____

Between stimulus and response, there is a space. In that space is our power to choose our response.
Viktor Frankl

Wednesday

Date:_____

First thing:

Can I stop for a moment and breathe? Notice my body and mind. How am I?

_____

_____

_____

_____

What calming activity or routine am I grateful for in my life?

_____

_____

_____

_____

Tip: Prioritising your own well-being is your best medicine.

End of the day:

Did I notice today anything that helped me be calm and regulated? Is there something I can try to introduce more of into my life?

_____

_____

_____

_____

Where did I find joy today? Is this usual or unusual? Why?

_____

_____

_____

_____

Mindfulness practices can reduce symptoms of stress, depression, and anxiety by 30% in teachers (Journal of Educational Psychology).

https://www.facebook.com/groups/preventingteacherburnout

Thursday

Date:_____

First thing:

How can I show kindness to someone today? Both to someone else and myself!

_____

_____

_____

_____

Do people in my home life understand what it's like to be working in a school? Could I explain it better to them? How?

_____

_____

_____

Tip: Boundaries are a form of self-respect and care.

End of the day:

Do I allow work to invade my home life, or have I set a clear boundary? What might I do better? How?

_____

_____

_____

_____

When today did I show myself some self-care and what did this look like? How can I increase this, even a small amount tomorrow?

_____

_____

_____

_____

Balance is not something you find, it's something you create.
Jana Kingsford

Friday

Rowena Hicks

Date:_____

First thing:

How are my energy levels this morning? Did I sleep enough?

_____

_____

_____

_____

How do I currently manage my emotions at work, and how can I improve?

_____

_____

_____

Tip: Sufficient rest and sleep are required to recharge your energy. Yes, it's better than chocolate!

End of the day:

When have I taken any moments to rest today? Have I? Do I think this is worth working on for next week, or not?

_____

_____

_____

_____

What was my best moment this week? Why am I so pleased with it?

_____

_____

_____

_____

Sleep quality can improve cognitive performance by 20%
(National Sleep Foundation).

https://www.facebook.com/groups/preventingteacherburnout

Weekend

Date:_____

First thing:

What moments from this week am I particularly grateful for, where I felt in control and balanced?

_____

_____

_____

Do I take care of my mental, physical, emotional and spiritual self? Enough?

_____

_____

_____

Tip: Celebrate Wins: Acknowledge and celebrate the progress you've made, no matter how small.

End of the day:

Do I notice if I am better regulated at home or work? Does one bounce off the other? How might I be able to detach them both?

_____

_____

_____

_____

Who do I know who is struggling and could really do with an encouragement today? How can I do this?

_____

_____

_____

_____

The key to success is to keep growing in all areas of life—mental, emotional, spiritual, as well as physical.
Julius Erving

https://www.facebook.com/groups/preventingteacherburnout

WEEK - 28

NAVIGATING ROUGH WATERS: FINDING STRENGTH AMIDST CHALLENGES

Monday

Date:_____

First thing:

Who am I most grateful to have in my life? In what ways do I appreciate them?

_____

_____

_____

What is my one biggest worry today? What is one tiny step that I can take to address it? Speak to someone? Break it down into smaller steps? Other?

_____

_____

_____

Tip: Embrace even the smallest wins.

End of the day:

What is one small win that I had today? What makes it a win?

_____

_____

_____

_____

What was my best moment today? Why was it good? Was it rest? Achievement? Connecting with someone? Exercise?

_____

_____

_____

_____

The journey of a thousand miles begins with one step.
Lao Tzu

https://www.facebook.com/groups/preventingteacherburnout

TEACH, FLOURISH,
THRIVE

Tuesday

Date:_____

First thing:

How does my body feel right now? Can I identify areas that feel stressed or tight? Jaw? Forehead? Shoulders? Take a moment to release them now. Better?

_____

_____

_____

How can I take ten minutes today for just ME self-care? What might this look like? Can I prioritise this? Do I believe this might help?

_____

_____

_____

Tip: Schedule "me time" in your planner as you would with any important meeting.

End of the day:

How did I do today with some ME time? Manage it? Results? If not, can I take a moment right now? What works best for me?

_____

_____

_____

_____

Which area in my life is going well right now? Healthy eating? Relationships? Health? Other? How does this impact my life positively?

_____

_____

_____

Research from the American Psychological Association indicates that regular self-care can reduce teacher burnout by up to 40%.

https://www.facebook.com/groups/preventingteacherburnout

Wednesday

Date:_____

First thing:

Who are my safe and trusted colleagues? What makes them safe for me?

_____

_____

_____

Which of these colleagues can I reach out to today? Have I been honest about how I feel? Do I believe the research that this will help me?

_____

_____

_____

Tip: Higher levels of social support are linked to lower levels of anxiety, emphasizing that social connections are critical for mental health. (2018). Current Psychiatry Reports, 20(2), 23.

End of the day:

When did I laugh today? How did it feel? If not enough, who makes me laugh that I could chat with tomorrow?

_____

_____

_____

_____

How did a conversation with a colleague help me today?

_____

_____

_____

_____

Alone we can do so little; together we can do so much.
Helen Keller

https://www.facebook.com/groups/preventingteacherburnout

Thursday

Date:_____

First thing:

Look around me right now. What is one item that attaches to a happy memory? What is it and how do I feel about it?

_____

_____

_____

Have I noticed this week when I have helped someone? A child? Colleague? Do I brush this off or can I start to take note? Even jot down the wins today?

_____

_____

_____

Tip: Internalise every time you make a positive impact on someone!

End of the day:

What are two small WINS I had today? These could be eating a healthier snack, having a short walk, finishing a task....

_____

_____

_____

_____

What positive impact did I have on someone today?

_____

_____

_____

_____

To the world, you may be just one person, but to one person, you may be the world.
Dr. Seuss

https://www.facebook.com/groups/preventingteacherburnout

Friday

Date:_____

First thing:

What three things am I grateful for this morning. Why did I choose these?

_____

_____

_____

_____

Who can I reach out to today who I know is struggling? When can I fit this in and what might work best?

_____

_____

_____

Tip: Positivity can be contagious!

End of the day:

Did I manage to reach out to that person who needs encouragement? How did it go and how did I feel?

_____

_____

_____

_____

Today, did I do something just for myself? Did I manage to take a few quiet moments? A lunch break? A chat? A walk? Did this help?

_____

_____

_____

_____

The more you praise and celebrate your life, the more there is
in life to celebrate.
Oprah Winfrey

https://www.facebook.com/groups/preventingteacherburnout

TEACH, FLOURISH,
THRIVE

Weekend

Date:_____

First thing:

I made it to Saturday. What moment over the last week am I most proud of? Why?

_____

_____

_____

_____

How can I rest and recharge this weekend? Do I know what helps me to re-charge best? What two things can I try?

_____

_____

_____

Tip: Give yourself permission to rest and recharge. Rest is productive.

End of the day:

How do I feel about how I have managed my challenges this week? What can I celebrate?

_____

_____

_____

_____

For next week, what is one thing I might try to do better or differently?

_____

_____

_____

_____

Rest and self-care are so important. When you take time to replenish your spirit, it allows you to serve others from the overflow.
Eleanor Brown

WEEK - 29

DARING TO BE MYSELF

Monday

Date:_____

First thing:

What am I looking forward to this coming week? Is it a good list?

_____

_____

_____

_____

What does it mean to me to be "myself"?

_____

_____

_____

Tip: Watch that you don't compromise your core beliefs.

End of the day:

Start small. Do I dare to share a piece of my authentic self with someone I trust? How can I do this and what might I say?

_____

_____

_____

_____

What is my biggest achievement today? How do I feel about it?

_____

_____

_____

_____

Authenticity is the daily practice of letting go of who we think we're supposed to be and embracing who we are.
Brené Brown

Rowena Hick

Date:_____

First thing:

Can I take a moment to notice how my body feels today? Do I know what works to help any areas of stress, tightness, pain?

_____

_____

_____

How do I feel this morning about whether I am accepted as me or do I feel judged? Does this surprise me to write it down like this?

_____

_____

_____

Tip: Fear of others' opinions is natural, but it shouldn't govern your actions or self-worth.

End of the day:

Can I identify one moment today when I felt judged? Consider how I can accept that feeling without letting it control me:

_____

_____

_____

_____

Write down five things that I am proud to have achieved or said so far this week. Does this remind me that I have strengths and skills?

_____

_____

_____

_____

To be yourself in a world that is constantly trying to make you something else is the greatest accomplishment.
Ralph Waldo Emerson

https://www.facebook.com/groups/preventingteacherburnout

TEACH, FLOURISH, THRIVE

Wednesday

Date:_____

First thing:

List three people I'm glad to do life with at the moment. Do I give back as much as they offer?

_____

_____

_____

Do I strive to be a perfectionist? If so, in a healthy way or is it damaging in some way?

_____

_____

_____

Tip: Perfection is a myth!

End of the day:

Is there one personal flaw I can recognise and address today? How can I see this as an area to celebrate, grow, learn or enjoy?

_____

_____

_____

_____

Where do I fit into the quote below? Am I proud of this? Could I describe myself in three words like this?

_____

_____

_____

_____

Imperfection is beauty, madness is genius and it's better to be absolutely ridiculous than absolutely boring.
Marilyn Monroe

Thursday

Date:_____

First thing:

How do I feel about myself this morning? Not about what I have achieved so far, but about me, who I am and how I turn up at the moment each day?

_____

_____

_____

Write about a time when I showed myself kindness and compassion:

_____

_____

_____

Tip: Kindness to yourself is as important as kindness to those around you.

End of the day:

When have I caught myself being self-critical today? Can I pause and reframe the thought with kindness and understanding?

_____

_____

_____

_____

What self-care activity have I prioritised today? How did it go? Can I build on it for tomorrow?

_____

_____

_____

_____

You are the most important project you will ever work on.
Louise Clarke

https://www.facebook.com/groups/preventingteacherburnout

Friday

Date:_____

First thing:

Today I am going to focus on self-validation. What does this mean to me and how can I benefit from it?

_____

_____

_____

Can I make one decision based solely on what feels right to me today, irrespective of others' thoughts? What might this be?

_____

_____

_____

Tip: Practice valuing your own opinion today.

End of the day:

Did I manage to make that one decision staying authentic to me today? How did it feel?

_____

_____

_____

_____

By practicing self-validation today, what are four things I've done to the best of my ability that I'm pleased with?

_____

_____

_____

_____

Don't let the noise of others' opinions drown out your own inner voice.
Steve Jobs

Weekend

Rowena Hick

Date:_____

First thing:

Reflect on what I have learned this week about embracing my authentic self. Write about my insights:

_____

_____

_____

How have my relationships been this week? Which one do I want to celebrate and invest in more?

_____

_____

_____

Tip: Your uniqueness is your strength!

End of the day:

Can I list an action I'm going to take in order to be more true to myself going forward?

_____

_____

_____

_____

Overall, has this week been a success for me? Why? When?

_____

_____

_____

_____

To thine own self be true.
William Shakespeare

https://www.facebook.com/groups/preventingteacherburnout

TEACH, FLOURISH, THRIVE

WEEK - 30
CLEAR THE CLUTTER

Monday

Date:_____

First thing:

What are the three biggest things that are using up my brain space right now? Use the sheets at the back to write a fuller list, if required.

_____

_____

_____

What is one thing or person I am grateful for today, that helps me reduce my stress? How does it / they help?

_____

_____

_____

Tip: It can help to write even the smallest stressors.

End of the day:

Have I noticed how I feel physically when I notice these stressors?

_____

_____

_____

_____

Can I take action to address even one small area of stress this week?

_____

_____

_____

_____

The greatest weapon against stress is our ability to choose one
thought over another.
William James

https://www.facebook.com/groups/preventingteacherburnout

Tuesday

Date:_____

First thing:

Who in my life makes me happy? Can I send them a quick message to tell them today?

_____

_____

_____

What task is most crucial to accomplish today? Why? How can I make it happen?

_____

_____

_____

Tip: Focus on what truly matters and let go of the rest. Prioritising can help reduce overwhelm.

End of the day:

What task did I complete today that made me feel accomplished?

_____

_____

_____

_____

Do I agree with today's quote? How does it make me feel?

_____

_____

_____

_____

It's not the load that breaks you down, it's the way you carry it.
Lou Holtz

https://www.facebook.com/groups/preventingteacherburnout

Wednesday

Date:_____

First thing:

What is really important to me today? Is it exercise? Time with family? Eating more healthily? Leaving on time? How can I make it happen?

_____

_____

_____

In what areas of my life do I currently feel overextended? How can I respectfully set a boundary in this area?

_____

_____

_____

Tip: Identify one area where you need to set a boundary and take action.

End of the day:

What went well for me today? Big or small - describe it, internalise the win:

_____

_____

_____

_____

What boundary did I set today that made me feel empowered?

_____

_____

_____

_____

You have to decide what your highest priorities are and have the courage—pleasantly, smilingly, unapologetically—to say 'no' to other things.
Stephen Covey

https://www.facebook.com/groups/preventingteacherburnout

Thursday

Date:_____

First thing:

What am I worrying about today? Can I ask someone to help me to sort one part?

_____

_____

_____

How can I incorporate more self-care into my routine?

_____

_____

_____

Tip: Watch who gets the best of you. Is that the right way round?

End of the day:

What self-care practice did I engage in today that restored my energy?

_____

_____

_____

_____

Do I believe the statistics about the importance of sometimes prioritising myself and does my daily routine reflect this?

_____

_____

_____

_____

The thing that is really hard, and really amazing, is giving up on being perfect
and beginning the work of becoming yourself.
Anna Quindlen

Friday

Date:_____

First thing:

Who am I able to encourage and support regularly? How does this make me feel?

_____

_____

_____

Who in my life provides me with the most support? How can I nurture this relationship further?

_____

_____

_____

Tip: A study from the University of North Carolina showed that strong social connections can reduce stress levels by up to 50%. Do I need to take action?

End of the day:

What connection or conversation today made me feel supported?

_____

_____

_____

How am I sleeping this week? How is my sleep routine? Have I tried writing down my main worries? Can I speak to someone? Try mindfulness?

_____

_____

_____

_____

We are all so much together, but we are all dying of loneliness.
Albert Schweitzer

https://www.facebook.com/groups/preventingteacherburnout

Weekend

Date:_____

First thing:

What have I learnt this week? My main takeaway? Am I prepared to learn and adapt?

_____

_____

_____

Can I take some time today to reflect on this past week and plan for next week, with a focus on finding some peace and prioritising certain tasks?

_____

_____

_____

Tip: It's brave to reflect, learn and then take action!

End of the day:

What am I proud of achieving this week?

_____

_____

_____

_____

When this week have I been at my best? Can I identify why and make sure I can replicate this next week?

_____

_____

_____

_____

The key to success is often the ability to adapt and reflect.
Anthony Robbins

https://www.facebook.com/groups/preventingteacherburnout

WEEK - 31
FINDING LAUGHTER AND JOY

Monday

Date:_____

First thing:

How do I feel this morning? How is my body and my mind? What one thing am I grateful for today?

_____

_____

_____

Who in my world really matters to me? Who needs some encouragement? How can I do this today?

_____

_____

_____

Tip: Focus on the little things that spark joy in your daily routine. Sometimes, it's the small moments that make the biggest difference.

End of the day:

What small joy am I most grateful for today?

_____

_____

_____

_____

What worked best in my day today?

_____

_____

_____

_____

Enjoy the little things, for one day you may look back and realise
they were the big things.
Robert Breault

https://www.facebook.com/groups/preventingteacherburnout

Tuesday

Date:_____

First thing:

Who makes me laugh? If I look at my week, when do I laugh most?

_____

_____

_____

Do I have a situation or issue that is reducing my joy right now? Is there a small step I can take today towards sorting it out or reducing it in some way?

_____

_____

_____

Tip: Laughter has been proven to reduce stress hormones like cortisol and adrenaline

End of the day:

What humorous moment today am I thankful for?

_____

_____

_____

_____

If I could imagine a moment of joy and laughter this week, what would I need to put into place? Can I make this happen, even a little?

_____

_____

_____

_____

Laughter is timeless, imagination has no age, and dreams are forever.
Walt Disney

Wednesday

Date:_____

First thing:

What playful activities that bring me joy and make me feel like a kid again can I engage in today? Is it worth trying to see the impact?

_____

_____

_____

Who do I know who would try some fun activity with me today? Otherwise, can I try something just for me that brings me joy? What?

_____

_____

_____

Tip: Dare to try something that brings you joy. You might be surprised!

End of the day:

What playful activity did I enjoy today? How did it make me feel more joyful?

_____

_____

_____

_____

How did my day go today? As expected? Can I bring a win to my mind and internalise how that felt?

_____

_____

_____

_____

We don't stop playing because we grow old; we grow
old because we stop playing.
George Bernard Shaw

Thursday

Date:_____

First thing:

Which friend do I share with most? Why am I grateful for them? What characteristics do I appreciate?

_____

_____

_____

Is there someone in my life who needs a bit of kindness today? Who? What could I do?

_____

_____

_____

Tip: Do something kind or joyful for someone else today – a small gesture can go a long way.

End of the day:

What act of kindness did I perform today that brought joy to another person? How did sharing joy make me feel?

_____

_____

_____

_____

How did experiencing joy today impact my overall mood and outlook?

_____

_____

_____

_____

The best way to cheer yourself is to try to cheer someone else up.
Mark Twain

Friday

Date:_____

First thing:

What has been my best moment so far this week? Why do I think it's my best?

_____

_____

_____

_____

What am I looking forward to today? Why?

_____

_____

_____

Tip: We all make mistakes but today is a new day!

End of the day:

When did I laugh today? Who was I with? How did this feel? How do I feel remembering it?

_____

_____

_____

_____

Can I go to sleep tonight thinking of the five things this week that have brought me joy?

_____

_____

_____

_____

Reflect upon your present blessings, of which every man has plenty; not on your past misfortunes, of which all men have some.
Charles Dickens

https://www.facebook.com/groups/preventingteacherburnout

Weekend

Date:_____

First thing:

How can I get out into nature, even for a short time this weekend?

_____

_____

_____

Can I review my journal entries from the week and identify patterns or themes in what brings me joy?

_____

_____

_____

Tip: Nature, laughter, exercise, friends…notice where you find joy.

End of the day:

What have I learned about finding joy this week? How can I continue to cultivate joy in my life moving forward?

_____

_____

_____

How many minutes have I been outside for this week? Enough? Can I increase it next week? What do I need to plan into my diary to make it happen?

_____

_____

_____

_____

A study by the University of Exeter Medical School found that spending at least 120 minutes a week in nature can improve overall well-being by 64%.

https://www.facebook.com/groups/preventingteacherburnout

226

WEEK - 32
CHANGING THE CONVERSATION

Date:_____

First thing:

What is a challenge I am facing this week? How does it feel?

_____

_____

_____

_____

Stopping for a moment, what five things can I see that bring me joy and peace around me?

_____

_____

_____

Tip: Embracing a "what" mindset opens doors to solutions and growth.

End of the day:

Have I tried today to shift my WHY questions to WHAT? Can I describe them? If not yet, can I re-frame an opportunity I missed today and prepare for tomorrow?

_____

_____

_____

_____

What went really well for me today? How did it feel?

_____

_____

_____

_____

Switching your mentality from "why is this happening to me?" to "what is this trying to teach me?" is a game changer.
Nelson Ishal Cruz

https://www.facebook.com/groups/preventingteacherburnout

Tuesday

Date:_____

First thing:

What challenge have I overcome recently? Do any key points stand out?

_____

_____

_____

_____

Can I identify a recurring "why" question in my thoughts and write an alternative "what" question here?

_____

_____

_____

Tip: Awareness is the first step towards change. Recognise the patterns holding you back.

End of the day:

Note three times today when I caught myself shifting from "why" to "what."

_____

_____

_____

_____

What really useful or joy-bringing conversation have I had today?

_____

_____

_____

_____

The quality of your life is determined by the quality of your questions.
Tony Robbins

Wednesday

Date:_____

First thing:

What am I looking forward to most today and why?

_____

_____

_____

_____

Can I reflect on a recent challenge? What did it teach me?

_____

_____

_____

Tip: Could this challenge be an opportunity?

End of the day:

In the situation I am in right now, can I see learning opportunities or possibilities for growth? Could I ask for help, training or resources?

_____

_____

_____

_____

What is something I have learnt about myself so far this week?

_____

_____

_____

_____

In the middle of difficulty lies opportunity.
Albert Einstein

https://www.facebook.com/groups/preventingteacherburnout

Thursday

Date:_____

First thing:

Is there one thing I can take action on today to help me overcome a situation?

_____

_____

_____

Write about a time when taking action helped me overcome a difficult situation:

_____

_____

_____

Tip: Taking action is brave, courageous, energy-inducing.

End of the day:

Did I take even a small step of action for myself, towards resolving a challenge today? If not, how can I plan for tomorrow?

_____

_____

_____

_____

Can I re-write one self-talk mantra I have right now? e.g. "I'm so exhausted, I can't do this" to "Although shattered, I'm going to plan in 15 minutes of self-care tomorrow"?

_____

_____

_____

_____

Do not wait to strike till the iron is hot; make it hot by striking.
William Butler Yeats

Friday

Date:_____

First thing:

What win have I had this week that I was not expecting?

_____

_____

_____

Describe a moment this week when I listened to what I needed and I took action to be kind to myself:

_____

_____

_____

Tip: Courage is to get up again after a failure or setback!

End of the day:

When did I manage to turn a WHY question into a WHAT question today? Did it help?

_____

_____

_____

_____

What one small, even tiny victory have I had this week? Describe it:

_____

_____

_____

_____

It does not matter how slowly you go as long as you do not stop.
Confucius

Weekend

Date:_____

First thing:

Looking at today's quote, repeated from Monday, what do I feel I've learnt?

_____

_____

_____

Reflect on this week's journey from "why" to "what." What changes have I noticed in my perspective?

_____

_____

_____

Tip: The questions we use can be game changing.

End of the day:

What has been my biggest accomplishment this week?

_____

_____

_____

_____

Have I engaged in some self-care and has it been effective? Do I need more? How can I make this happen?

_____

_____

_____

_____

Switching your mentality from "why is this happening to me?" to "what is this trying to teach me?" is a game changer.
Nelson Ishal Cruz

https://www.facebook.com/groups/preventingteacherburnout

WEEK - 33
RETRAINING MIND AND BODY

Monday

Date:_____

First thing:

How is my body feeling this morning?

_____

_____

_____

_____

What three things am I looking forward to the most this week?

_____

_____

_____

_____

Tip: **Watch for positive things around me.**

End of the day:

Did setting my mind on positive things help to start my week in a good way? What positives can I remember from my day?

_____

_____

_____

_____

Can I have thirty minutes of screen-free time before I go to sleep this week? Watch this week for the impact!

_____

_____

_____

_____

It is not the strongest of the species that survive, nor the most intelligent, but the one most responsive to change.
Charles Darwin

https://www.facebook.com/groups/preventingteacherburnout

Tuesday

Date:_____

First thing:

When I walk into class this morning, watch what happens if I stand straight, shoulders back, take a deep breath. What do I think might happen?

_____

_____

_____

If I feel exhausted, I can tell myself to release the thought pattern and body weariness. As I breathe out now, I will say "Let go!" five times. Does this help?

_____

_____

_____

Tip: Confuse your brain today!

End of the day:

What happened when I walked into class this morning?

_____

_____

_____

_____

Have I managed to release some of the overwhelm and tension today? What did it feel like in my body?

_____

_____

_____

_____

Strength does not come from physical capacity. It comes from an indomitable will.
Mahatma Gandhi

https://www.facebook.com/groups/preventingteacherburnout

Wednesday

Date:_____

Rowena Hicks

First thing:

How did I sleep last night, having spent the day yesterday focusing on releasing the tension in my body?

_____

_____

_____

_____

What are two things I am looking forward to today?

_____

_____

_____

Tip: Holding tension in our body is exhausting!

End of the day:

How does my body feel right now? Did I practice releasing tension today? Have I noticed any improvement?

_____

_____

_____

_____

What is one thing I can do tonight, to add to my thirty minutes of non-screen time, that will help me sleep?

_____

_____

_____

_____

Your body can stand almost anything. It's your mind that you have to convince.
Unknown

CH, FLOURISH, THRIVE

Thursday

Date:_____

First thing:

Who are three people I'm grateful to have in my life? Why?

_____

_____

_____

_____

Today, can I stand straight and tell myself I have the energy for a great day? What else can I do to make my brain think "I've got this"?

_____

_____

_____

Tip: A huge percent of your communication is through your body language.

End of the day:

As I watched my body language today, what difference did it make on my relationships and communication?

_____

_____

_____

_____

When today did I feel confident? How do I feel about this?

_____

_____

_____

_____

Actions speak louder than words. Let your words teach and your actions speak.
Anthony of Padua

https://www.facebook.com/groups/preventingteacherburnout

Friday

Date:_____

First thing:

How does my body feel this morning? Compare it to Monday or last Friday? Has being more aware of the tension I hold reduced it?

_____

_____

_____

_____

What one child or adult looks like they are struggling this week? How can I step in for them today?

_____

_____

_____

Tip: Treating your mind kindly is as important as treating your body well.

End of the day:

What have I gained from being more aware of the tension in my body this week, and addressing it?

_____

_____

_____

_____

What strategies have worked for me this week?

_____

_____

_____

_____

The body achieves what the mind believes.
Unknown

Date:_____

First thing:

Can I list any other strategies I am aware of that release tension in my body?

_____

_____

_____

_____

What two things do I agree to action this weekend as self-care to reduce my stress?

_____

_____

_____

Tip: Committing oneself to releasing tension can impact our mind and our body!

End of the day:

How does my body feel tonight? What has helped me most this week?

_____

_____

_____

_____

What are my three biggest wins this week overall?

_____

_____

_____

_____

The way we communicate with others and with ourselves ultimately determines the quality of our lives.
Tony Robbins

https://www.facebook.com/groups/preventingteacherburnout

WEEK - 34

TOGETHER WE THRIVE: CULTIVATING AWARENESS FOR OTHERS

Monday

Date:_____

First thing:

Which three people am I grateful for today and why?

_____

_____

_____

Do I feel listened to? Who hears me well? How do I feel when someone really listens?

_____

_____

_____

Tip: In a recent study, 70% of participants responded to feeling reduced stress when focusing on helping others that week in some way.

End of the day:

Have I managed to effectively listen to someone today? How did I feel and what about them?

_____

_____

_____

_____

What was my best moment today? Why was it the best?

_____

_____

_____

_____

Listening is an art that requires attention over talent, spirit over ego, others over self.
Dean Jackson

Tuesday

Date:_____

First thing:

How do I feel today about focussing on being kind to others? How can this help me if I feel overwhelmed already?

_____

_____

_____

Who do I know who needs some encouragement today? Can I make a plan now? What can I do? Coffee? Leave a note on their desk? Text?

_____

_____

_____

Tip: Even the smallest act of kindness can transform that person's day!

End of the day:

How did my day go? Am I proud of any particular moments in my day? Why?

_____

_____

_____

_____

Have I been kind to myself at all today? If so, how? If not, how can I make sure I add something into my day tomorrow?

_____

_____

_____

_____

No act of kindness, no matter how small, is ever wasted.
Aesop

Wednesday

Date:_____

First thing:

How does my body feel this morning? Am I carrying stress in my shoulders, jaw, elsewhere? Can I take a moment to describe this and then to simply relax and breathe?

_____

_____

_____

Who can I reach out to who I haven't connected with in a while and check on how they're doing? Why might this also be good for me?

_____

_____

_____

Tip: We need others in our life to be able to live our best selves.

End of the day:

What was my most meaningful conversation today? What made is so?

_____

_____

_____

_____

Where today did I show myself to be resilient? Even something small:

_____

_____

_____

_____

The most basic and powerful way to connect to another
person is to listen. Just listen.
Rachel Naomi Remen

https://www.facebook.com/groups/preventingteacherburnout

Thursday

Date:_____

First thing:

What have I done well so far this week? A task, relationship, kindness?.....

_____

_____

_____

How do I feel about focussing on giving genuine words of kindness to others? Do I receive these myself?

_____

_____

_____

Tip: A compliment is verbal sunshine. Robert Orben

End of the day:

When I gave a compliment today, how did the other person react and how did I feel?

_____

_____

_____

_____

How exhausted am I at the moment? Am I sleeping enough? What is one thing I can do to increase my sleep time or the quality of my sleep?

_____

_____

_____

_____

Kind words can be short and easy to speak, but their echoes are truly endless.
Mother Teresa

Friday

Date:_____

First thing:

Who in my world do I like spending time with? Can I identify what it is about them that makes them an attractive and energy-filling person to be around?

_____

_____

_____

Who around me is struggling this week? How might I be able to help them? Even the smallest thing:

_____

_____

_____

Tip: Acts of support can significantly reduce stress levels in both the giver and receiver.

End of the day:

Did I manage to support someone else today? How did this feel for me?

_____

_____

_____

_____

What five lovely, small moments did I have today?

_____

_____

_____

_____

We rise by lifting others.
Robert Ingersoll

Weekend

Date:_____

First thing:

How would I describe this week? Have there been any small changes I can notice for the better?

_____

_____

_____

_____

Can I do an emotional check-in for myself and one other person (who?) today? Start with me - how am I? Really?

_____

_____

_____

Tip: Be the reason someone smiles today!

End of the day:

Who else did I check-in on today? Did it help for me to do this for them?

_____

_____

_____

_____

What is my biggest win from this week? Can I replicate something similar next week?

_____

_____

_____

_____

What do we live for, if it is not to make life less difficult for each other?
George Eliot

WEEK - 35
PRACTICAL STEPS TO TAKE WHEN OVERWHELMED

Monday

Date:_____

First thing:

What was my big win of last week? Was it work or home related? Can I describe how this feels?

_____

_____

_____

_____

Can I create a to-do list and prioritise tasks by importance and urgency? Focus on completing the most critical ones first.

_____

_____

_____

Tip: Prioritising tasks increases productivity.

End of the day:

Did I tackle something urgent and important today, even if just one thing? Was creating a prioritised list helpful?

_____

_____

_____

_____

Which three people am I grateful for today? Why?

_____

_____

_____

_____

You don't have to see the whole staircase, just take the first step.
Martin Luther King Jr.

Tuesday

Date:_____

First thing:

What am I looking forward to this week?

_____

_____

_____

_____

What is one boundary I am prepared to put in place for my day today? Leaving on time? Proper lunch break? Explain why I am unable to do something?

_____

_____

_____

Tip: Setting boundaries enables us to be the best version of ourselves.

End of the day:

How did I get on with just one boundary today? Did it impact others? Was that OK? How do I feel about it?

_____

_____

_____

_____

What was a conversation I had today where I smiled as did they?

_____

_____

_____

_____

Daring to set boundaries is about having the courage to love ourselves even when we risk disappointing others.
Brené Brown

Wednesday

Date:_____

First thing:

What have I done so far this week that would come under the heading of self-care. Does this list surprise me? Is it good or does it need work?

_____

_____

_____

_____

What can I plan into my day today, so I ensure a better level of self-care than yesterday? How can I manage this if I am so so busy?

_____

_____

_____

Tip: Start small - try fifteen minutes of self-care today!

End of the day:

Did my self-care focus make any improvements today? If I haven't managed much today, can I take five minutes now?

_____

_____

_____

_____

Have I encouraged anyone today? Who around me needs it? Who could I focus on tomorrow? How?

_____

_____

_____

_____

Self-care is not a waste of time; self-care makes your use of time more sustainable.
Jackie Viramontez

https://www.facebook.com/groups/preventingteacherburnout

Thursday

Date:_____

First thing:

How am I getting on with my list? Is it still overwhelming or have I made progress, or both?

_____

_____

_____

How do I feel about asking for help with something on my to-do list? Can I see it as a sign of self-care rather than weakness? Shall I go for it today?

_____

_____

_____

Tip: Asking for help is a sign of strength!

End of the day:

Did I ask for help today? How did it go? Did someone ask me for help? How did that feel?

_____

_____

_____

_____

Can I write down three things I know I am good at. Could I help someone else using one of these strengths?

_____

_____

_____

You can do anything, but not everything. Asking for help allows you to focus on what you do best.
Tim Ferriss

https://www.facebook.com/groups/preventingteacherburnout

Friday

Date:_____

First thing:

What is one thing that has worked well for me this week?

_____

_____

_____

_____

Is there one area at work that I can make more simple? What is one small step I can take towards this today to make this more efficient?

_____

_____

_____

Tip: Simplicity is the ultimate sophistication. Leonardo da Vinci

End of the day:

What went well today? Was it planned?

_____

_____

_____

_____

Can I take a mindful moment? Put on some reflective music and notice what I am grateful for this week? Even the smallest things count.

_____

_____

_____

_____

Complexity is your enemy. Any fool can make something complicated. It is hard to keep things simple.
Richard Branson

Weekend

Date:_____

First thing:

As I reflect on the past week, what are the wins that stand out most to me?

_____

_____

_____

_____

What self-care activities have I booked in for this weekend? Is that enough? How do I even define self-care for myself?

_____

_____

_____

Tip: Celebrate what you want to see more of. Tom Peters

End of the day:

What steps have helped me this week to manage and even to see moments of thriving?

_____

_____

_____

_____

Am I taking care of my sleep? Do I prioritise a healthy sleep routine? Do I allow myself enough hours of sleep? Anything I need to change?

_____

_____

_____

_____

It's the little details that are vital. Little things make big things happen.
John Wooden

https://www.facebook.com/groups/preventingteacherburnout

WEEK - 36
RECOGNISING YOUR STRENGTHS

Date:_____

First thing:

This week is about our strengths! What are my three most valued strengths that I bring to my role?

_____

_____

_____

_____

Do I dare ask three trusted friends or colleagues what they think are my three most valued strengths to them and why? Who will I ask?

_____

_____

_____

Tip: In order to be the best version of you, you need to be using your most valued strengths in your role!

End of the day:

How did today go? Did anything surprise me?

_____

_____

_____

_____

Where did I use my strengths? Did I notice how I was feeling in these times?

_____

_____

_____

_____

Recognising your strengths allows you to leverage your natural talents
and live a more fulfilling life.
Stephen Covey

Tuesday

Date:_____

First thing:

In the last couple of weeks, what has gone really well? Was I using my valued strengths at the time?

_____

_____

_____

_____

What am I looking forward to today? Why?

_____

_____

_____

Tip: Your past successes are proof of your capabilities.

End of the day:

Can I create a "success list" of at least five past achievements and identify the strengths I used for each?

_____

_____

_____

_____

_____

_____

_____

_____

Recognising your strengths builds your confidence and gives you the courage to face any obstacle.
Oprah Winfrey

Wednesday

Date:_____

First thing:

Can I write three lines of kindness to myself? Is this how I generally speak to myself?

_____

_____

_____

_____

Write about three qualities I appreciate in myself when I'm under stress.

_____

_____

_____

_____

Tip: Giving yourself grace under pressure is itself a strength.

End of the day:

Which of my strengths did I use today? When?

_____

_____

_____

_____

Did I take a minimum of fifteen minutes of self-care today?

_____

_____

_____

_____

Understanding your unique strengths is key to unlocking your full potential.
Tony Robbins

https://www.facebook.com/groups/preventingteacherburnout

Thursday

Date:_____

First thing:

How is my body feeling today? Can I take a moment to relax it, breathe slowly and take notice?

_____

_____

_____

Which of my strengths will I plan to use today? Is this easy or do I need to make adjustments to ensure I fit it in?

_____

_____

_____

Tip: Engage in an activity today that allows you to use one of your top strengths.

End of the day:

Did I notice a time when I felt resilient today?

_____

_____

_____

_____

Who did I connect with today? Was it accidental or purposeful? Did it help?

_____

_____

_____

_____

Noticing our strengths helps us appreciate the power and
resilience we hold within.
Brené Brown

https://www.facebook.com/groups/preventingteacherburnout

Friday

Date:_____

First thing:

Can I list three small wins from this week? Home or work?

_____

_____

_____

_____

What have I surprised myself by achieving this week? Even the smallest thing matters!

_____

_____

_____

Tip: Celebrate the small as well as the obvious wins!

End of the day:

Have I noticed my strengths more this week? How does this help me?

_____

_____

_____

_____

How can I treat myself in a way that feels rewarding this weekend – a simple act of self-care to acknowledge my strengths and achievements this week?

_____

_____

_____

_____

When we recognise our strengths, we empower ourselves to tackle challenges
with confidence and clarity.
Unknown

https://www.facebook.com/groups/preventingteacherburnout

Weekend

Date:_____

Rowena Hicks

First thing:

As I recognise my strengths, has this helped my confidence? How?

_____

_____

_____

_____

What am I looking forward to most this weekend?

_____

_____

_____

_____

Tip: Keep noticing the wins. It confuses your brain away from the negatives.

End of the day:

As I reflect back on my week, what am I proud of?

_____

_____

_____

_____

What moment of joy this week do I want to plan to replicate next week?

_____

_____

_____

_____

Success is achieved by developing our strengths, not by
eliminating our weaknesses.
Marilyn vos Savant

https://www.facebook.com/groups/preventingteacherburnout

WEEK - 37

PATHWAYS TO PURPOSE: REFLECTING ON OUR CHOICES

Monday

Date:_____

First thing:

As I look at my choices this week, can I reflect on a positive choice I made in my teaching career. How did it impact me and my students?

_____

_____

_____

Every choice I've made has brought me to this moment. Which life choices have I made that I celebrate in particular?

_____

_____

_____

Tip: Take time to recognise the power in your everyday decisions, no matter how small they seem.

End of the day:

Do I agree with the quote below, or do I feel like sometimes life has happened to me and not been a choice?

_____

_____

_____

_____

What went well for me today? Can I list three things that made me smile? Even small things like someone giving me a smile, a hug or a coffee?

_____

_____

_____

_____

Life is the sum of all your choices.
Albert Camus

https://www.facebook.com/groups/preventingteacherburnout

Tuesday

Date:_____

First thing:

What am I grateful for in this coming day?

_____

_____

_____

_____

What do I have a choice about today? Which direction am I going to go?
Why?

_____

_____

_____

**Tip: Start each morning by setting an intention for one positive choice
you will make throughout the day.**

End of the day:

What is one choice I made today that positively impacted my day?

_____

_____

_____

_____

I know that connection is so important. Have I taken time to build
connection with someone today in a meaningful way? If not, how can I
tomorrow?

_____

_____

_____

_____

Choose wisely, for we become what we repeatedly do.
Sean Covey

https://www.facebook.com/groups/preventingteacherburnout

Wednesday

Date:_____

First thing:

Can I feel excited this morning about a long-term goal I have? Can I write it here and what choice or choices I need to make to achieve it?

_____

_____

_____

Can I write a healthy choice I can make this morning to build my energy and productivity? It can be something quite small:

_____

_____

_____

Tip: Write down your long-term professional goals and the choices you need to make to achieve them.

End of the day:

What decision did I make today that felt empowering, that sat well with me, or set a boundary of self-care?

_____

_____

_____

_____

Looking at the quote below, am I making choices that show who I truly am? Have I made choices that don't sit well with me? What is one small step I can take to adjust this?

_____

_____

_____

_____

It is our choices, Harry, that show what we truly are, far more than our abilities.
J.K. Rowling

Thursday

Date:_____

First thing:

How would I describe my mind this morning? Peaceful? Cluttered? Busy? Focussed? What is one thing I'm looking forward to today?

_____

_____

_____

Identify a challenging situation where a wise choice led to a positive outcome:

_____

_____

_____

Tip: Facing challenges is part of the journey. Every challenge you overcome through choice strengthens your resilience.

End of the day:

What challenge did I face today, or am I currently facing? What choices do I have in response?

_____

_____

_____

_____

Have I made any healthy choices for myself today? Perhaps a moment of self-care, or healthy food options or seeking a quiet moment with a friend?

_____

_____

_____

_____

Difficulties are things that show a person what they are.
Epictetus

TEACH, FLOURISH,
THRIVE

Friday

Date:_____

First thing:

What is one decision I can make right now to put myself first today?

_____

_____

_____

_____

Where have I had a win so far this week? Was it a surprise?

_____

_____

_____

Tip: Prioritising your well-being is a choice that benefits not only you but also those around you.

End of the day:

Did I manage to put myself first at any point today? What did this look like? How do I feel about it?

_____

_____

_____

_____

At the end of this week, what are three small things I managed to do, that perhaps other people may not notice?

_____

_____

_____

_____

Your life changes the moment you make a new, congruent, and committed decision.
Tony Robbins

https://www.facebook.com/groups/preventingteacherburnout

Weekend

Date:_____

First thing:

As I look back on my choices this week, do I feel stronger for having reflected more on each of them?

_____

_____

_____

_____

Can I give myself permission this weekend to put myself first, even for a few minutes, so I have some quality self-care to re-charge my batteries?

_____

_____

_____

Tip: Regularly review and celebrate your positive choices to reinforce your ability to make impactful decisions.

End of the day:

Can I look forward to next week? What choices and decisions do I have coming up? What do good outcomes look like for me?

_____

_____

_____

_____

Did today just happen to me or was it the outcome of choices? How can I ensure tomorrow involves some good, healthy and restful choices?

_____

_____

_____

_____

Life is a matter of choices, and every choice you make makes you.
John C. Maxwell

WEEK - 38
MY IMPACT!

Monday

Date:_____

First thing:

Can I remember a reason or two why I came into teaching?

_____

_____

_____

_____

Can I recall a recent moment when I made a positive and significant impact on a student or colleague?

_____

_____

_____

_____

Tip: Research shows that 78% of students remember a teacher who made a positive impact on their lives.

End of the day:

This week, I agree to take note daily of two times when I have made a positive impact on a student or colleague:

_____

_____

_____

_____

In acknowledgement of ME, I hereby tell myself that I will do one small thing each day to prioritise what I need. What can I do tomorrow?

_____

_____

_____

_____

They may forget what you said, but they will never forget how you made them feel.
Carl W. Buehner

Tuesday

Date:_____

First thing:

This morning, how is my self-talk? Do I believe I can have a great day?
Can I write a short sentence of how I can manage it?

_____

_____

_____

_____

Can I list two ways that I help my workplace to tick over and function
effectively?

_____

_____

_____

Tip: You are a crucial cog in the school machine!

End of the day:

Again, here I agree to take note daily of two times when I have made a
positive impact on a student or colleague:

_____

_____

_____

_____

What are three achievements from today that no one else noticed?

_____

_____

_____

_____

Simply by being yourself and sharing your gifts, skills, empathy, kindness and
courage you will impact the children and your team.
Rowena Hicks

Buy My Book Here: www.rowenahicks.com/books

Date:_____

First thing:

Do I believe I offer a gift to the children I teach, support, believe in, encourage? How?

_____

_____

_____

_____

Which of my team is struggling to understand the impact they are having at the moment? How can I encourage them today?

_____

_____

_____

Tip: Let's agree to celebrate ourselves and the wins of others!

End of the day:

Again, here I agree to take note daily of two times when I have made a positive impact on a student or colleague:

_____

_____

_____

_____

Write a sentence to myself explaining what a great job I do and the impact I have:

_____

_____

_____

_____

I want to remind you that if you work in a school, you have such an immense impact on the children you support!
Rowena Hicks

Thursday

Date:_____

First thing:

Can I reflect for a quick moment on what I'm really good at? My valued strengths. When might I be able to use these today?

_____

_____

_____

_____

What am I most looking forward to today?

_____

_____

_____

Tip: We all have such value. We just need to SEE it!

End of the day:

Again, here I agree to take note daily of two times when I have made a positive impact on a student or colleague:

_____

_____

_____

_____

How do I feel tonight? Can I notice any areas of stress in my body and relax these areas? What else can I do to help my mind and body switch off?

_____

_____

_____

Whatever your role, you contribute to the well-oiled machine of school life!
Rowena Hicks

Buy My Book Here: www.rowenahicks.com/books

Friday

Date:_____

First thing:

In Rowena Hicks' book, she talks about drains and radiators. Do I have these in my team? Who are the best radiators? How can I connect with them today?

_____

_____

_____

When have I made good decisions this week? Can I see any positive impact?

_____

_____

_____

Tip: Watch today, even if exhausted, am I still a radiator?

End of the day:

Again, here I agree to take note daily of two times when I have made a positive impact on a student or colleague:

_____

_____

_____

_____

When did I laugh today? Who with?

_____

_____

_____

_____

Surround yourself with only people who are going to lift you higher.
Oprah Winfrey

Weekend

Date:_____

First thing:

Have I started to see more of the impact I have? Has anything surprised me?

_____

_____

_____

_____

Have I noticed where I fit in and how I can also support those around me? How have I managed to do this?

_____

_____

_____

Tip: Even the small things matter.

End of the day:

How does it make me feel to have logged a number of big or small times where I had a positive impact on those in my world?

_____

_____

_____

_____

What am I most proud of and why?

_____

_____

_____

_____

The more you praise and celebrate your life, the more there is
in life to celebrate.
Oprah Winfrey

WEEK - 39
ORGANISE, PRIORITISE, ACHIEVE!

Monday

Date:_____

First thing:

New week, new start. What three things am I looking forward to this week and why?

_____

_____

_____

What are the most important tasks I need to accomplish this week, and why are they important?

_____

_____

_____

Tip: Are your tasks today or this week important, urgent or both?

End of the day:

Did I do things that are truly important to me today, or were they important to others? How do I feel about these things?

_____

_____

_____

_____

How can I put myself first in just one thing this week? How do I feel about doing this? Selfish? Frustrated? Relieved? Given permission? ... WHY?

_____

_____

_____

_____

The key is not to prioritise what's on your schedule, but to schedule your priorities.
Stephen Covey

https://www.facebook.com/groups/preventingteacherburnout

Tuesday

Date:_____

First thing:

What was the main thing on my mind when I woke up today? Does this tell me I am anxious, relaxed, happy…. How can I address this today?

_____

_____

_____

_____

What is one small thing I can do today to encourage someone else?

_____

_____

_____

Tip: Break down large tasks into smaller pieces to make them less overwhelming and more actionable.

End of the day:

Do I feel like I am getting any jobs done that feel important at the moment? If not, what small step can I take?

_____

_____

_____

_____

What am I most pleased about achieving today and why?

_____

_____

_____

_____

The journey of a thousand miles begins with one step.
Lao Tzu

https://www.facebook.com/groups/preventingteacherburnout

Wednesday

Date:_____

First thing:

Which task can I turn into a SMART goal this week, and what is my plan to achieve it?

_____

_____

_____

_____

Am I feeling on top of my to-do list at the moment? Can I list here for today my most important and my most urgent task?

_____

_____

_____

Tip: Use the SMART criteria (Specific, Measurable, Achievable, Relevant, Time-bound) to set clear and attainable goals.

End of the day:

Did I achieve any steps towards achieving my goal for this week? If not, what happened? If yes, what is the next small step I can plan in?

_____

_____

_____

_____

Imagine it is the end of term. What is the main thing I want to have achieved that is on my list at the moment?

_____

_____

_____

_____

Set your goals high and don't stop until you get there.
Bo Jackson

Thursday

Date:_____

First thing:

Who am I grateful for in my life at the moment? Why?

_____
_____
_____
_____

Am I easily distracted? What are my main sources of distraction? Can I do anything about any of them?

_____
_____
_____

Tip: Find those distractions and show them the door, so you can keep your productivity alive and kicking!

End of the day:

Did I manage to minimise any distractions today? What worked and what didn't?

_____
_____
_____
_____

Write about a time I showed kindness to someone else. How did it make me feel, and how can I incorporate more acts of kindness into my life?

_____
_____
_____
_____

You will never reach your destination if you stop and throw stones at
every dog that barks.
Winston Churchill

Friday

Date:_____

First thing:

What is one positive intention I can set for the day? How will I focus on implementing this intention?

_____

_____

_____

_____

So far, has this week been productive or a struggle, or both? Can I reflect on why?

_____

_____

_____

Tip: Reflection is a key to progress.

End of the day:

What has worked well this week? What can I improve on next week?

_____

_____

_____

_____

Who showed me kindness this week? How did I feel when this happened? Was it small, big, common, a surprise? What can I learn from this?

_____

_____

_____

_____

Without reflection, we go blindly on our way.
Margaret J. Wheatley

Weekend

Date:_____

First thing:

How do I feel about what I achieved this week? Be honest: what am I pleased with and what am I frustrated about? Any actions as a result?

_____

_____

_____

_____

Did I have a WIN this week that surprised me? Can I replicate this next week in some way?

_____

_____

_____

Tip: Celebrating your wins, no matter how small, boosts your confidence and motivation.

End of the day:

Have I taken some time for me today? Do I have boundaries around my work times? Where have I achieved this well?

_____

_____

_____

_____

What tasks am I celebrating completing this week? Are these at home or work? Which am I most proud of?

_____

_____

_____

_____

The more you celebrate your life, the more there is in life to celebrate.
Oprah Winfrey

WEEK - 40
CULTIVATING A SENSE OF ENOUGH:
EMBRACING ADEQUACY

Monday

Date:_____

First thing:

What is an area in which I am confident? Have I always been confident in this? Is there more than one area?

_____

_____

_____

_____

What is an area in which I feel less confident? Can I describe why?

_____

_____

_____

Tip: Start to notice the WINS in your day!

End of the day:

Do I feel like I have to prove things to people? What does this look like in practice?

_____

_____

_____

_____

What were my three biggest wins today?

_____

_____

_____

_____

You alone are enough. You have nothing to prove to anybody.
Maya Angelou

Tuesday

Date:_____

First thing:

Can I list my three most valued strengths and three things I'm most confident at within my job?

_____

_____

_____

What task am I worrying about today? Who can I talk to who will understand and help me to find a solution?

_____

_____

_____

Tip: Google JOHARI's WINDOW. Note that each window is not a set size. As you grow, the windows shrink or grow with you.

End of the day:

What are two things that are in window 2 from Johari? Those things that I know about myself that I don't want others to know:

_____

_____

_____

_____

Who helped me today and who did I support? Was this refreshing? Helpful?

_____

_____

_____

_____

I have revealed that I have had times where I have felt inadequate and what I've done about it....as I have shared this I have become empowered and feel stronger as a result.
Rowena Hicks

Buy My Book Here: www.rowenahicks.com/books

Wednesday

Date:_____

First thing:

Do I have a colleague or friend who is really struggling at the moment? How can I reach out? A text? A note on their desk? Make a coffee for them?

_____

_____

_____

Can I write here a sentence about what I CAN achieve today, that I am strong enough, I do have energy, I know I am needed and appreciated?

_____

_____

_____

Tip: Watch your self-talk. Turn it on its head if necessary.

End of the day:

Look at the list of affirmations at the back of this journal. Cut one out for this week and continue to cut them out as needed. Which is my favourite today?

_____

_____

_____

_____

List three times I managed when it became challenging in some way today:

_____

_____

_____

_____

You are braver than you believe, stronger than you seem, and smarter than you think.
A.A. Milne

Thursday

Date:_____

First thing:

Thinking about my team, what skills do I bring that others may not be so strong in? What particular strengths do I offer?

_____

_____

_____

Is there an area I feel less confident in, that a team member could support me with? How do I feel about asking?

_____

_____

_____

Tip: We are stronger together!

End of the day:

Can I think of a challenge that I could turn into an opportunity? Does this feel too much? Do-able? Maybe I can ask for help with this?

_____

_____

_____

_____

How does my body feel tonight? Am I holding stress in areas? Can I take a moment to breathe, listen to waves crashing on a beach? Now describe me!

_____

_____

_____

_____

In the middle of every difficulty lies opportunity.
Albert Einstein

Date:_____

First thing:

How do I feel about giving myself even a small moment of self-compassion? Does this feel impossible with the load? How can I fit it in?

_____

_____

_____

What small habit can I adapt today that will help me feel I have a little control and help me to be better organised?

_____

_____

_____

Tip: Small, even tiny steps can be so powerful.

End of the day:

Have I managed a small bit of ME-TIME today? Do I know what works best for me? Am I starting to understand that this is really important for me?

_____

_____

_____

_____

Looking at my week, what three things am I most proud of? Why?

_____

_____

_____

_____

Success is the sum of small efforts repeated day in and day out.
Robert Collier

Weekend

Date:_____

First thing:

Who do I have a healthy, reciprocal friendship with? Is there one particular aspect of this friendship that is important to me?

_____

_____

_____

Who do I know who is a real encouragement to me, who I'd like to build a stronger friendship with? How can I achieve this?

_____

_____

_____

Tip: Watch to see if your friends raise you up or pull you down.

End of the day:

Do I invest enough time in my friendships? How can I build on this over this weekend?

_____

_____

_____

_____

Do I feel like I have achieved something meaningful this week? It can even be a small thing for one person. List as many as I can:

_____

_____

_____

_____

Friendship is born at that moment when one person says to another, 'What! You too? I thought I was the only one.
C.S. Lewis

WEEK - 41
THE MANY FACES OF SCHOOL RELATIONSHIPS

Monday

Date:_____

First thing:

What is going well in life right now? What can I celebrate to start my week?

_____

_____

_____

Write about a time when a colleague's support made a big difference in my day:

_____

_____

_____

Tip: Set aside a few minutes today to have a meaningful conversation with a colleague.

End of the day:

Taking note of the study result below, which colleagues do I have the most healthy relationships with and why?

_____

_____

_____

_____

Who do I know that I would like to build a better friendship with? How can I do that this week?

_____

_____

_____

_____

According to a study by the American Psychological Association, teachers who have strong collaborative relationships with colleagues report being more satisfied with their jobs and less stressed.

https://www.facebook.com/groups/preventingteacherburnout

Tuesday

Date:_____

First thing:

Am I sleeping well and eating well? Would I say I'm looking after myself well enough? Could I improve one small thing today?

_____

_____

_____

What was a win I had yesterday with a student? How did I feel?

_____

_____

_____

Tip: Reflect on a memorable moment with a student that made you feel appreciated.

End of the day:

Did I have time to ask any students how they really are today? Why does this matter?

_____

_____

_____

_____

What have I done today for me to look after myself? Is it enough?

_____

_____

_____

_____

To teach is to touch a life forever.
Unknown

Wednesday

Date:_____

First thing:

If I look out of a window now, what do I notice? Describe five things:

_____

_____

_____

_____

When did I last collaborate with a colleague and what were the benefits?

_____

_____

_____

Tip: Benefits of collaboration include providing fresh perspectives and reduced feelings of isolation.

End of the day:

Which colleague might I be able to collaborate with to help me overcome some of the overwhelming tasks right now? What could this look like?

_____

_____

_____

_____

How is my sleep? Is it healthy? Am I on my phone right before I sleep? Do I have a regular routine that helps? Is there one thing I can adjust?

_____

_____

_____

_____

Coming together is a beginning; keeping together is progress; working together is success.
Henry Ford

https://www.facebook.com/groups/preventingteacherburnout

Thursday

Date:_____

First thing:

Have I had some good conversations so far this week? Describe my best:

_____

_____

_____

_____

How are my boundaries around work relationships with students, parents and colleagues?

_____

_____

_____

Tip: Notice how you communicate in difficult situations. Are you regulated?

End of the day:

How is my boundary-setting around my professional and personal relationships? Good enough?

_____

_____

_____

_____

Who or what made my day today? How and why?

_____

_____

_____

_____

Boundaries are a part of self-care. They are healthy, normal, and necessary.
Doreen Virtue

Friday

Date:_____

First thing:

Which of my colleagues can I encourage today? How can I support them?

_____

_____

_____

In view of today's quote, do I take on too much responsibility and worry for the children in my care?

_____

_____

_____

Tip: Celebrate good relationships; they are a gift, not to be taken for granted.

End of the day:

What student or colleague did I positively impact today and how?

_____

_____

_____

_____

How do I feel about the quality of my relationships at work?

_____

_____

_____

_____

It takes a village to raise a child.
African Proverb

https://www.facebook.com/groups/preventingteacherburnout

Weekend

Date:_____

First thing:

Can I list three key relationships I have and describe what they offer me in one word each?

_____

_____

_____

Can I describe four key relationships I have and describe what I offer each of them in one word?

_____

_____

_____

Tip: Relationships take intentional investment.

End of the day:

Can I describe a really useful or surprisingly good conversation I had this week?

_____

_____

_____

_____

Can I take a few minutes now to switch off and help my brain unwind? What helps me best to do this? Note it down then do it!

_____

_____

_____

_____

Education is a shared commitment between dedicated teachers, motivated students and enthusiastic parents with high expectations.
Bob Beauprez

https://www.facebook.com/groups/preventingteacherburnout

WEEK - 42
HOW TO SYNC WORK AND LIFE

Monday

Date:_____

First thing:

What are my priorities this week? Are they only mine? How can I make sure I fit these into my busy schedule?

_____

_____

_____

_____

How do I feel this week about looking at where I and my needs fit into the planner?

_____

_____

_____

Tip: Remember a moment of rest is so important in a busy day!

End of the day:

When today did I fit in any self-care, relaxation or rest? Is it enough? What can I improve on for tomorrow? How?

_____

_____

_____

_____

What was my biggest win today? Was it expected?

_____

_____

_____

_____

The key is not to prioritise what's on your schedule, but to schedule your priorities.
Stephen Covey

https://www.facebook.com/groups/preventingteacherburnout

Tuesday

Date:_____

First thing:

Who are five people that I am so grateful for right now?

_____

_____

_____

_____

How do I feel about risking the disappointment of others if I gently tell them I am not able to do something for them? i.e.- I am saying NO.

_____

_____

_____

Tip: Saying No to something today may be your biggest win.

End of the day:

Today, did I demonstrate to myself that I love myself by any of my actions? When?

_____

_____

_____

_____

Is there a boundary or a fence that I can set up in order to take better care of myself?

_____

_____

_____

_____

Good fences make good neighbours.
Robert Frost

Wednesday

Date:_____

First thing:

How am I feeling this morning? Do I feel like I need to do a lot of work on my balance between home and work?

_____

_____

_____

_____

How is my time management? What is working and what is not?

_____

_____

_____

Tip: Do the worst job first!

End of the day:

Did I accomplish the most important and urgent things on my list today? If not, how can I plan to do so tomorrow?

_____

_____

_____

_____

What in my day today gave me a sense of achievement and purpose?

_____

_____

_____

_____

The bad news is time flies. The good news is you're the pilot.
Michael Altshuler

https://www.facebook.com/groups/preventingteacherburnout

Thursday

Date:_____

First thing:

What does my support network look like at the moment? Is there someone I would like to link up with who could be a healthy addition to this group?

_____

_____

_____

Which part of my job is giving me the most energy right now: relationships, meaning, accomplishment, engagement or emotions?

_____

_____

_____

Tip: Positive well-being requires positive relationships!

End of the day:

Can I ask around to find people's best top tips for improving their efficiency? What are mine?

_____

_____

_____

_____

What was my best conversation from today? Why was it my best?

_____

_____

_____

_____

Ask a colleague how they are, not about their work.
Rowena Hicks

Buy My Book Here: www.rowenahicks.com/books

Friday

Date:_____

First thing:

What aspects of my job do I enjoy the most and why?

_____

_____

_____

Reflect on a time when I efficiently managed a heavy workload. What strategies did I use?

_____

_____

_____

Tip: Break down your tasks into smaller, manageable chunks and focus on completing them one at a time.

End of the day:

What three things are heavily weighing on me from my workload right now? Is there one thing I can plan to take action on to reduce this? Even a small thing?

_____

_____

_____

_____

When in my day today did I feel joy, or flow or feel as though I was really doing well? What was I doing? Was I using a valued strength?

_____

_____

_____

_____

You may need to go proactively looking for those things that fill you, on those days that have a will of their own and go in a draining direction.
Rowena Hicks

Buy My Book Here: www.rowenahicks.com/books

Weekend

Date:_____

First thing:

Reflecting on the past week, which of my strengths have stood out most in managing my work-life balance?

_____

_____

_____

_____

If the quote below is right, I need to take some small yet achievable steps towards achieving a better balance. What are two steps for today?

_____

_____

_____

Tip: You need confidence to stand up for yourself.

End of the day:

When today did I make a decision to put myself and my needs first? How did this feel? If I'm not sure I did, how can I do so tomorrow?

_____

_____

_____

_____

Is there something on my mind that is worrying me at the moment that I could ask for help with? If so, what and who and how can I do this?

_____

_____

_____

_____

Balance is not something you find, it's something you create.
Jana Kingsford

https://www.facebook.com/groups/preventingteacherburnout

WEEK - 43
STRESS BUSTING!

Monday

Date:_____

First thing:

Write about three things I am grateful for despite feeling stressed:

_____

_____

_____

_____

Can I identify my top three stressors and consider how I can address them one step at a time?

_____

_____

_____

Tip: Acknowledging stress and stressors is the first step to managing them.

End of the day:

Looking at the quote below, what have I done recently that I really enjoyed and that brought me energy, laughter, joy?

_____

_____

_____

_____

How do I usually react to stress? Are these reactions helpful or harmful?

_____

_____

_____

_____

You are not stressed because you are doing too much. You are stressed because you are doing too little of what makes you feel most alive.
Ahmed Hankir

https://www.facebook.com/groups/preventingteacherburnout

Tuesday

Date:_____

First thing:

What am I looking forward to in my day today? Even the smallest thing can shift my focus:

_____

_____

_____

_____

As I listen to my body this morning, where do I sense or feel stress? Can I take a moment to breathe into those spaces? Send oxygen to give them energy?

_____

_____

_____

Tip: Your body gives you clues when something isn't right. Listen to it and take care.

End of the day:

Note moments today when I felt physically healthy or energised:

_____

_____

_____

_____

What can I try tonight to help my mind to switch off? A meditation app? A novel? Soothing music? Hot bath? Can I give myself this gift?

_____

_____

_____

_____

Tension is who you think you should be. Relaxation is who you are.
Chinese Proverb

https://www.facebook.com/groups/preventingteacherburnout

Wednesday

Date:_____

First thing:

When have I recently felt emotionally balanced and peaceful? Was it a moment or an activity?

_____

_____

_____

Identify one emotional symptom of stress today and try to address it through my favourite coping strategy, like talking to a friend and journaling it here:

_____

_____

_____

Tip: Describing how you feel helps to process it.

End of the day:

How would I describe how I feel tonight? Is it emotional exhaustion? Is it compassion fatigue? What sorts of words describe it best?

_____

_____

_____

_____

What went really well in my day today? Why?

_____

_____

_____

_____

The greatest weapon against stress is our ability to choose one
thought over another.
William James

https://www.facebook.com/groups/preventingteacherburnout

Thursday

Date:_____

First thing:

Who has helped me this week and who have I been able to help?

_____

_____

_____

_____

Think of a time when my mind felt clear and focussed. What was I doing?

_____

_____

_____

Tip: Your thoughts do NOT define you!

End of the day:

Do I feel as though I have brain fog? Can I take a few minutes to practice mindfulness, remind myself of my achievements and let my thoughts go?

_____

_____

_____

_____

How do I feel about the quote below? Is that me?

_____

_____

_____

_____

Stress is caused by being 'here' but wanting to be 'there'.
Eckhart Tolle

Friday

Date:_____

First thing:

What healthy habit do I have that I'm thankful for? How does it help me?

_____

_____

_____

_____

Can I identify one positive behaviour to replace a negative stress-induced habit, such as taking a walk instead of reaching for unhealthy snacks?

_____

_____

_____

Tip: Small changes to habits go a long way!

End of the day:

Can I take a small bit of control back in my day? What new habit can I practice that could reduce my stress? Even a five-minute lunch break is a start!

_____

_____

_____

_____

Can I describe one, short moment of joy or peace in my day today?

_____

_____

_____

_____

You must learn to let go. Release the stress. You were never in control anyway.
Steve Maraboli

Weekend

Date:_____

First thing:

As I reflect on my journey this week, how would I describe what I've learned about managing stress?

_____

_____

_____

_____

I have the power to create a plan that works for me and reduces my stress. What are the two main action points?

_____

_____

_____

Tip: Remember to lean on those around you. Don't isolate yourself.

End of the day:

What are two things I've taken on board this week from journaling?

_____

_____

_____

_____

What has been my biggest win this week? Have I shared it with someone?

_____

_____

_____

_____

Anxiety does not empty tomorrow of its sorrows, but only empties today of its strength.
Charles Spurgeon

WEEK - 44

LONGER HOLIDAY

Monday

Date:_____

First thing:

This week I am thinking about whether I have managed to unplug as I enter the holidays. How have I managed to disconnect from work so far? Have I?

_____

_____

_____

What are the two main issues I have swirling around in my head? Can I take a small step today towards sorting these?

_____

_____

_____

Tip: Can I score how good at boundaries I am at the start of this week?

End of the day:

What boundaries do I need to put in place this week in order to protect myself and allow my brain to unplug?

_____

_____

_____

_____

What has gone well today and what am I most excited for this week?

_____

_____

_____

_____

Almost everything will work again if you unplug it for a few
minutes, including you.
Anne Lamott

https://www.facebook.com/groups/preventingteacherburnout

312

Tuesday

Date:_____

First thing:

Is my head still whizzing with "stuff" this morning? What is the main thing and why?

_____

_____

_____

_____

Can I take two minutes to put work related stuff on a list and then add it to a drawer in my mind's cabinet? When shall I open that drawer again?

_____

_____

_____

Tip: Focus on YOU and see what happens!

End of the day:

What did I do today that has best helped me to start to unwind? Why was it helpful?

_____

_____

_____

Who around me gives me energy, or makes me feel good? Can I book to see them this week?

_____

_____

_____

_____

Sometimes the most productive thing you can do is relax.
Mark Black

Wednesday

Date:_____

First thing:

Have I found peace from the ups and downs of last term? Am I holding on to something I shouldn't?

_____

_____

_____

_____

How does my body feel today? Am I holding tension anywhere? What can I do to release this through today?

_____

_____

_____

Tip: Looking after ourselves in mind and body isn't selfish!

End of the day:

What steps have I taken today to start to properly look after my body and has it helped?

_____

_____

_____

_____

What is one win I had today? Can I share it with someone who would enjoy it?

_____

_____

_____

_____

Take care of your body. It's the only place you have to live.
Jim Rohn

https://www.facebook.com/groups/preventingteacherburnout

Thursday

Date:_____

First thing:

What 3 things do I feel grateful for this morning?

_____

_____

_____

_____

How can I be purposeful about filling my own cup, so I allow my mind and body to properly unwind today?

_____

_____

_____

Tip: Being physically active helps us sleep!

End of the day:

Did I do things that made me laugh today? How did that feel? Can I get more of it tomorrow?

_____

_____

_____

_____

How am I doing to unwind so far this week? Am I being kind to myself?

_____

_____

_____

_____

The reason I exercise is for the quality of life I enjoy.
Kenneth H. Cooper

Friday

Date:_____

First thing:

Am I starting to see my best self again? What are the qualities I'm most proud of that I see in myself at the moment?

_____

_____

_____

_____

What has gone well this week that I am proud of? Can I replicate it?

_____

_____

_____

Tip: Putting ourselves first is essential to be the best we can for others.

End of the day:

Am I doing things at the moment because I want to do them or because others want me to do them? Honestly?

_____

_____

_____

_____

What are three things I am grateful that I have in my life right now? Why?

_____

_____

_____

_____

Self-care is giving the world the best of you, instead of what's left of you.
Katie Reed.

https://www.facebook.com/groups/preventingteacherburnout

Weekend

Date:_____

First thing:

Do I feel peaceful about life? What am I proud of?

_____

_____

_____

_____

Have I said no to things this week that didn't sit well with me? How does this feel?

_____

_____

_____

Tip: What is my boundaries score at the end of this week, compared to the start?

End of the day:

What is one example of where I have put MYSELF first this week? How does this feel?

_____

_____

_____

_____

Who has encouraged me this week and who have I encouraged? Can I do more of this? With whom?

_____

_____

_____

_____

Daring to set boundaries is about having the courage to love ourselves, even when we risk disappointing others.
Brené Brown

WEEK - 45
SURVIVING HOLIDAY HAVOC

Monday

Date:_____

First thing:

What are three things I am grateful for today despite the busy schedule?

_____

_____

_____

If I look at my schedule for this week, am I doing things that are for me, or have I agreed to do things for others that will drain me? Is everything good?

_____

_____

_____

Tip: Does being busy make you feel successful or exhausted?

End of the day:

Have I taken a few moments to be mindful, pause and relax today? Did it help? If not, can I do that right now? Reflect on how I feel in my body, my breathing:

_____

_____

_____

_____

Even if I'm busy, can I still have a healthy sleep routine? What does this look like for me? Am I on my phone too much? Can I watch this for the week?

_____

_____

_____

_____

Mindfulness isn't difficult; we just need to remember to do it.
Sharon Salzber

https://www.facebook.com/groups/preventingteacherburnout

Tuesday

Date:_____

First thing:

Amidst the busyness, how calm does my mind feel?

_____

_____

_____

_____

What self-care activity can I commit to today, even if it's just for a few minutes?

_____

_____

_____

Tip: Schedule a short activity that you enjoy and that relaxes you, such as reading or listening to music.

End of the day:

Have I been calm through all the busy times today?

_____

_____

_____

_____

Who do I know who is really good at staying calm and balanced? How do they do it? Is it worth a chat to find out? Do I want a bit more of that calm?

_____

_____

_____

_____

Your calm mind is the ultimate weapon against your challenges.
Bryant McGill

Wednesday

Date:_____

First thing:

How do I feel about trying for a healthy day today? What might this look like? Do I need to change a habit I have?

_____

_____

_____

_____

What am I really looking forward to today? If I can't think of something, what can I add to my planner right now?

_____

_____

_____

Tip: Incorporate a short exercise routine or walk to stay active.

End of the day:

Has today been a healthy day for me? What has made it so? Can I adapt something for tomorrow to take another step forwards in this area?

_____

_____

_____

Do I feel contented at the end of today? What do I feel about my habits overall?

_____

_____

_____

_____

Health is the greatest possession. Contentment is the greatest treasure.
Lao Tzu

Thursday

Date:_____

First thing:

What are three things I'm grateful for today?

_____

_____

_____

_____

If I'm on holiday, am I starting to unplug and recharge? What is holding me back if not? What are my indicators that I am starting to relax?

_____

_____

_____

Tip: Watch for what is working well right now - even small things.

End of the day:

What results can I see from my recent hard work? Has it been seen and validated? Does this make a difference to me?

_____

_____

_____

_____

Who around me needs some encouragement? How can I do that? How do I feel to focus on their needs and how I can help?

_____

_____

_____

_____

Sometimes it takes only one act of kindness to change a person's life.
Jackie Chan

Friday

Date:_____

First thing:

Do I feel any stress round my body today? Neck? Jaw? Stomach? How can I address this need to reduce pressure on my body (and mind) today?

_____

_____

_____

What do I truly enjoy doing that brings me peace?

_____

_____

_____

Tip: Plan a small, calming activity like a nature walk or a hot bath.

End of the day:

How do I feel about today's quote? Do I agree? What action, even small steps, can I take to address this going forward?

_____

_____

_____

_____

Am I hard on myself? How is my self-talk? Would I talk to my friend in the way I speak to myself? Can I write a short sentence to myself that affirms me today?

_____

_____

_____

_____

The time to relax is when you don't have time for it.
Sydney J. Harris

Weekend

Date:_____

First thing:

What might a day of rest look like for me?

_____

_____

_____

_____

How is my emotional balance at the moment? Is there something I can do to take action to support this part of me?

_____

_____

_____

Tip: Dedicate part of your day to doing something peaceful and restorative.

End of the day:

When is one time today that I found peace? How can I make that happen more often?

_____

_____

_____

_____

Can I list three things that boost my energy?

_____

_____

_____

_____

A single day of rest can boost mental clarity and emotional balance by 40%.
Medical News Today.

https://www.facebook.com/groups/preventingteacherburnout

WEEK - 46
UNPLUG, UNWIND AND RECHARGE

Monday

Date:_____

First thing:

What has been the best thing about the holidays so far? Why is it top?

_____

_____

_____

_____

Are there two boundaries I can set for this holiday? How can I communicate these to the relevant people?

_____

_____

_____

Tip: Taking time for yourself is not a luxury, it's a necessity. You deserve to recharge.

End of the day:

When did I laugh most today, or at least feel most relaxed? How can I plan to have more of that this week?

_____

_____

_____

_____

Have I managed to put in place a boundary? Examples could be: out of office onto emails, unplug time, take emails off my phone, not over-committing my time.

_____

_____

_____

_____

Saying no can be the ultimate self-care.
Claudia Black

https://www.facebook.com/groups/preventingteacherburnout

TEACH, FLOURISH,
THRIVE

Tuesday

Date:_____

Rowena Hicks

First thing:

What are my three top fun activities I want to make sure I do this holiday? How can I make sure they happen?

_____

_____

_____

How does my body feel this morning? Do I feel like I am relaxing well? Can I do more? Can I take a moment to breathe right now, let shoulders fall, breathe again:

_____

_____

_____

Tip: Planning ahead helps make room for the things that truly matter.

End of the day:

Am I being realistic about the things I want to achieve this holidays or am I stressing just to try to fit them in? What can I change?

_____

_____

_____

_____

What are my three top priorities of jobs that need to be completed before the end of the holidays? Can I schedule them into my diary?

_____

_____

_____

_____

To accomplish great things, we must not only act, but also dream; not only plan, but also believe.
Anatole France

https://www.facebook.com/groups/preventingteacherburnout

H, FLOURISH, THRIVE

Wednesday

Date:_____

First thing:

What activities help me feel rested and relaxed? How can I incorporate more of these activities into my holiday schedule?

_____

_____

_____

So far this week, what have I enjoyed the most? Is this because of people or things? Can I organise more of this?

_____

_____

_____

Tip: Schedule downtime in your calendar.

End of the day:

Who am I grateful for today? Why?

_____

_____

_____

_____

What did I do today that helped me to relax the most? What was the opposite? Tomorrow, can I make sure I focus on the former option?

_____

_____

_____

_____

Sometimes the most productive thing you can do is relax.
Mark Black

https://www.facebook.com/groups/preventingteacherburnout

Thursday

Date:_____

Rowena Hicks

First thing:

What physical activities do I enjoy that can fit into my holiday routine? How do these activities make me feel more energised?

_____

_____

_____

Am I managing to keep a healthy and balanced diet this holiday? Can I set up a plan to manage this better? Where do I start?

_____

_____

_____

Tip: A little movement each day can bring a lot of extra energy.

End of the day:

Have I managed a balance of different types of relaxation today? Is that exercise, stopping, fun with friends, others? What seems to have the greatest impact for me?

_____

_____

_____

_____

How have I supported someone else today? How did I feel? Was I still being true to myself in this time?

_____

_____

_____

_____

Exercise not only changes your body, but it also changes your mind, your attitude, and your mood.
Unknown

https://www.facebook.com/groups/preventingteacherburnout

H, FLOURISH, THRIVE

Friday

Date:_____

First thing:

How has taking time to reflect impacted my mood and outlook?

_____

_____

_____

_____

What is working this holiday to help me recharge my batteries? What isn't?

_____

_____

_____

Tip: Gratitude turns what we have into enough.

End of the day:

List five things I'm so grateful to have in my life right now. What is their impact on me?

_____

_____

_____

_____

Am I grateful for everything or are there tough things going on too? Can I see any beads of hope within them to focus my mind on?

_____

_____

_____

_____

Gratitude is the fairest blossom which springs from the soul.
Henry Ward Beecher

https://www.facebook.com/groups/preventingteacherburnout

Weekend

Date:_____

First thing:

Looking back on my week, how did I do? Achieve much? Enjoy a lot? Relax well? Eat and exercise enough? Be honest!

_____

_____

_____

Can I set a small goal for next week to try to improve on one or two of the above areas? How can I do this? Be specific:

_____

_____

_____

Tip: Each day is a new beginning. Embrace the fresh starts.

End of the day:

What one new thing that I haven't tried before can I attempt next week? Maybe cook something new? Go somewhere different? Try a new sport?

_____

_____

_____

_____

Who in my life right now brings me joy? Why is this? How can I increase this with more people?

_____

_____

_____

_____

Goal setting is one of the most powerful motivational tools.
Edwin A Locke

WEEK - 47

A WEEK OFF...PHEW!

Monday

Date:_____

First thing:

What am I most excited about doing this week?

_____

_____

_____

_____

Reflect on a moment where I positively impacted a student's learning or confidence:

_____

_____

_____

Tip: Rest is not a luxury; it's a necessity. Embrace it wholeheartedly.

End of the day:

Today, have I done something purely for relaxation like reading a book, taking a walk, or listening to my favourite music? Can I do more of this tomorrow?

_____

_____

_____

_____

Have my batteries started to re-charge? How do I rest best and how can I book this into my week?

_____

_____

_____

_____

According to the American Psychological Association, taking regular breaks can reduce stress and improve productivity by up to 40%.

https://www.facebook.com/groups/preventingteacherburnout

Tuesday

Date:_____

First thing:

How is my to-do list for this week? Is there one thing I can plan to take action on today to relieve worry about something?

_____

_____

_____

Do I have a self-care ritual, or can I start one today, in which I can start to help myself unplug and unwind?

_____

_____

_____

Tip: Self-care is giving the world the best of you, not what's left of you.

End of the day:

Where did I find joy today?

_____

_____

_____

When, how and where do I find it easiest and most productive to properly rest? How can I add more of this into this week? Can I? Is it important?

_____

_____

_____

Research shows that engaging in self-care activities can decrease anxiety and depression by 30-40%.

TEACH, FLOURISH, THRIVE

Wednesday

Date:_____

First thing:

Can I remember what made me fall in love with teaching? Does that passion still burn within me? All the time? At certain times?

_____

_____

_____

On this week off, what can I do that I LOVE doing? What hobbies or activities build me up and energise me? Can I book them in? Be intentional?

_____

_____

_____

Tip: Your passion is your fuel. Let it remind you why you do what you do.

End of the day:

What activity today energised me? Was this when I felt joy the most or was that another activity?

_____

_____

_____

How is my sleep at the moment? Is there anything I can do to prioritise more, deeper sleep? Less screen time? More exercise? Better bedtime routine?

_____

_____

_____

Passion is energy. Feel the power that comes from focusing on what excites you.
Oprah Winfrey

Thursday

Date:_____

First thing:

Can I name a friend who I am grateful for today? Can I see them this week? How can I also encourage them this week?

_____

_____

_____

Over the past month, which three people have I connected with in a mutually beneficial way? Can I send them a message to say "Thank you? I appreciate you"?

_____

_____

_____

Tip: Teachers who have strong professional relationships are 25% less likely to experience burnout, according to Education Week.

End of the day:

Have I had meaningful chats today? Do I need to prioritise this for tomorrow?

_____

_____

_____

How are my energy and mood levels? Am I managing to unplug from work? Is there one thing I could do to help me unwind tomorrow?

_____

_____

_____

Your network is your net worth.
Porter Gale

https://www.facebook.com/groups/preventingteacherburnout

Friday

Date:_____

First thing:

Can I list ten people and / or things I am grateful for right at this moment?

_____

_____

_____

_____

If gratitude is a mood buster, how can I turn over a challenge and see it another way? Can I re-write the narrative here, now?

_____

_____

_____

Tip: Gratitude is a mood buster!

End of the day:

What went really well today and what is one thing I would have changed?

_____

_____

_____

How is my body feeling tonight? If I notice each part, how would I describe it? Do I need to take a moment to deep breathe? Perhaps stop and reflect?

_____

_____

_____

Gratitude turns what we have into enough.
Aesop

https://www.facebook.com/groups/preventingteacherburnout

Weekend

Date:_____

First thing:

What has been the best part of my week so far? Why was it so good?

_____

_____

_____

Today, can I spend some time goal-setting for the term ahead, including prioritising my own well-being and self-care in this?

_____

_____

_____

Tip: Planning ahead with a rested mind brings clarity and purpose.

End of the day:

How do I feel about planning ahead? Am I where I want to be? Do I have a longer term goal for myself?

_____

_____

_____

_____

What is one new healthy habit I will try to start for next week? Do I need to prepare anything ahead to make this happen?

_____

_____

_____

_____

The best way to predict your future is to create it.
Abraham Lincoln

WEEK - 48
LAST WEEK OF THE HOLIDAYS

Monday

Date:_____

First thing:

What was the most rewarding experience I had over the holidays? How can I bring that sense of joy and fulfilment into my classroom?

_____

_____

_____

_____

When have I laughed most during this holidays? Can I replicate that sort of situation this week? How?

_____

_____

_____

Tip: Laughter triggers the release of endorphins, the body's natural feel-good chemicals.

End of the day:

Where have my thoughts been focused today? Positive or negative?

_____

_____

_____

_____

What three things am I grateful for today?

_____

_____

_____

_____

The joy we feel has little to do with the circumstances of our lives and everything to do with the focus of our lives.
Russell M. Nelson

https://www.facebook.com/groups/preventingteacherburnout

340

Tuesday

Date:_____

(Rowena Hicks)

First thing:

What's one goal I have for the new term? What steps can I take to achieve it, and how can I track my progress?

_____

_____

_____

_____

Looking at the coming term, what am I looking forward to the most?

_____

_____

_____

_____

Tip: With well-defined goals, you can create actionable plans.

End of the day:

Have I planned some time just for myself this week? Enough?

_____

_____

_____

_____

If I have a worry about this coming term, what is it and who can I share it with?

_____

_____

_____

_____

Setting goals is the first step in turning the invisible into the visible.
Tony Robbins

Wednesday

Date:_____

First thing:

Think about a challenge I faced last term. How did I overcome it, and what did I learn from the experience?

_____

_____

_____

_____

How do I respond to challenge in general? Am I kind to myself and balanced in my response?

_____

_____

_____

Tip: Believe in your ability to overcome the challenge!

End of the day:

What challenge am I facing right now? How can I re-think it in my mind so it can have a positive outcome?

_____

_____

_____

_____

What friend do I know who has a challenge, who I can contact to offer a supportive encouragement? Do I have the energy for this?

_____

_____

_____

_____

The greatest glory in living lies not in never falling, but in rising every time we fall.
Nelson Mandela

https://www.facebook.com/groups/preventingteacherburnout

Thursday

Date:_____

First thing:

List three ways I can make an impact on the students I meet this coming term:

_____

_____

_____

_____

Which three colleagues am I excited to be working with? Why them?

_____

_____

_____

_____

Tip: Thinking about our impact helps us focus on the positives.

End of the day:

In what ways do I see that I make a difference in my role?

_____

_____

_____

_____

What is one thing I can do tomorrow to help boost my energy?

_____

_____

_____

_____

Education is the most powerful weapon which you can use to change the world.
Nelson Mandela

Friday

Date:_____

First thing:

List three things I am grateful for in my teaching career and explain why each one is important to me:

_____

_____

_____

_____

When I think about the coming term, what makes me excited?

_____

_____

_____

Tip: Your joy is contagious!

End of the day:

How does my body feel today? Am I carrying stress or pain, can I help it to relax more?

_____

_____

_____

_____

Do I have a healthy sleep routine? Do I need to look into this and the benefits for myself? What might help me?

_____

_____

_____

_____

Gratitude turns what we have into enough.
Aesop

Weekend

Date:_____

First thing:

Think about one aspect of teaching that brings me joy. How can I bring more of this joy into my daily routine?

_____

_____

_____

_____

Who do I know who needs support or encouragement at the moment? How can I connect today to help lift their spirits?

_____

_____

_____

Tip: Acts of kindness and helping others can boost your own happiness.

End of the day:

Have I noticed how I am impacted as I help or reach out to others?

_____

_____

_____

_____

Can I shift my focus from my concerns for the coming term towards what I am grateful for this term? What are my two top people, things or activities I'm grateful for looking forward?

_____

_____

_____

Find a place inside where there's joy, and the joy will burn out the pain.
Joseph Campbell

WEEK - 49

START OF THE HOLIDAYS

Monday

Date:_____

First thing:

What was my biggest win at school last term? Why?

_____

_____

_____

_____

What am I most looking forward to this holiday? Why is this first on my list? How can I make sure it happens?

_____

_____

_____

Tip: Reaching out to someone to say thank you can make their day and also make yours!

End of the day:

Today was I the best version I can be of myself? When was I at my best?

_____

_____

_____

As I start the holidays, can I start a new habit that will help me start to sleep? What can I agree with myself to try? e.g. turn off my phone thirty___ minutes before bed, practice a relaxing pre-sleep routine.

_____

_____

_____

_____

Every decision, setback, or triumph is an opportunity to identify the seeds of truth that make you the wondrous human being you are.
Oprah Winfrey

Tuesday

Date:_____

First thing:

If I agree today will have some self-care elements for me to unwind, what can I try today?

_____

_____

_____

What about one lovely moment for each of my physical, mental and emotional wellbeing? Can I plan it into my day?

_____

_____

_____

Tip: Self-care refers to the practice of taking deliberate action!

End of the day:

What went well today? Did I manage to take deliberate action? If not, what got in the way?

_____

_____

_____

_____

What three words describe how my body feels tonight? Do I need to take a few breaths or relax my jaw? Can I identify what I'm holding onto, if anything?

_____

_____

_____

_____

Self-care is not selfish. You cannot serve from an empty vessel.
Eleanor Brown

Wednesday

Date:_____

First thing:

Which people in my life am I grateful for today? Why?

_____

_____

_____

I know connection is important. Who can I connect with today who is a priority for me? Is this a mutual friendship / relationship? How?

_____

_____

_____

Tip: Relationships provide encouragement and motivation, making it easier to bounce back from setbacks and face life's challenges with confidence.

End of the day:

Have I managed to connect with someone in a meaningful way today? How did this go?

_____

_____

_____

_____

Can I name one person in my life who really SEES me? And who do I do this for? Why does this even matter?

_____

_____

_____

_____

Connection is the energy that is created between people when they feel seen, heard, and valued - when they can give and receive without judgment.
Brené Brown

Thursday

Date:_____

First thing:

How did I sleep last night? Score out of 10? Is this my regular pattern and how do I feel about it?

_____

_____

_____

What am I looking forward to today? Have I booked in something for my physical, emotional and mental wellbeing? If not, what can I add?

_____

_____

_____

Tip: Laughter and sleep are basic human requirements.

End of the day:

When did I laugh most today? How can I set up situations tomorrow where I make sure I laugh more?

_____

_____

_____

_____

How am I doing with a bedtime routine? We tell children in our classes it's important; what about me? How can I improve mine? Am I willing to try this new habit? Try it for a week then review?

_____

_____

_____

_____

A good laugh and a long sleep are the best cures in the doctor's book.
Irish Proverb

TEACH, FLOURISH, THRIVE

Friday

Date:_____

First thing:

How do I feel about having a healthy day today? What does this mean for me?

_____

_____

_____

_____

Can I score my emotional health, physical health, spiritual health, environmental, social and mental health out of 10? Watch these today…

_____

_____

_____

Tip: We need to care for all areas of ourselves.

End of the day:

Which area of my health is most healthy? What could I focus on tomorrow and how?

_____

_____

_____

_____

What went really well today? Why was it good? Who benefitted? What can I learn from this to repeat going forward?

_____

_____

_____

_____

It is health that is real wealth and not pieces of gold and silver.
Mahatma Gandhi

Weekend

Date:_____

First thing:

Am I feeling less stressed today than at the start of the week? What has helped and what hasn't?

_____

_____

_____

_____

Have I managed to turn off my work emails, notifications and reduce my screen time? Has it helped? How does this feel? Does it even help me?

_____

_____

_____

Tip: Taking time for self-care can enhance productivity and focus.

End of the day:

Have I managed to start to unwind? What does this mean for me? Have I unplugged yet?

_____

_____

_____

_____

My best moment this week? Why was it so good?

_____

_____

_____

_____

Almost everything will work again if you unplug it for a few minutes, including you.
Anne Lamott

WEEK - 50

HELP, I CAN'T SWITCH OFF!

Monday

Date:_____

First thing:

How am I feeling today in three words? Then how is my body feeling?
Can I slow my breathing right now and relax my body? Any better?

_____

_____

_____

As I get to decide who I spend time with this week, who are my priorities
and why? Have I booked them in to my schedule?

_____

_____

_____

Tip: Love yourself enough to set boundaries.

End of the day:

Have I met one of my own needs today? Do I even know what I need?
Can I explain here?

_____

_____

_____

_____

What was my favourite part of today? Why am I grateful for it?

_____

_____

_____

_____

The only people who get upset about you setting boundaries are the ones who
were benefitting from you having none.
Morewithless

Tuesday

Date:_____

First thing:

Describe a peaceful moment I have had recently, in detail:

_____

_____

_____

_____

How is my sleep at the moment? Can I Google some strategies today to try out this week to help me switch off? What comes up for me to try?

_____

_____

_____

Tip: A bedtime routine is proven to increase quality of sleep.

End of the day:

When have I laughed today? Can I get more of this during this week?

_____

_____

_____

_____

How would I describe my sleep routine? Is it helping me to switch off my mind and relax my body?

_____

_____

_____

_____

A good laugh and a long sleep are the best cures in the doctor's book.
Irish Proverb

Wednesday

Date:_____

First thing:

Am I starting to switch off? What are the main barriers to being able to do this?

_____

_____

_____

Can I see on my phone how long I've been spending on it each day this week? Then add laptop and TV and any other screen. Am I surprised by the total?

_____

_____

_____

Tip: Set a tech curfew an hour before bed. Try it! It's harder than you think.

End of the day:

What is my favourite non-screen activity? Can I do more of this? Can I see in what way this is good for me?

_____

_____

_____

_____

The Beatles sang: Turn off your mind, relax, and float downstream. How can I relax tonight to help me find peace and calm and rest?

_____

_____

_____

_____

An article from Harvard Health notes that blue light from screens can interfere with the production of melatonin, a hormone crucial for sleep. Reducing screen time before bed can help restore natural sleep patterns.

https://www.facebook.com/groups/preventingteacherburnout

Thursday

Date:_____

First thing:

How do I feel about increasing my exercise today? What are the benefits I see or do I relate to the quote below?

_____

_____

_____

What is my favourite form of exercise? Why do I enjoy it and how do I benefit?

_____

_____

_____

Tip: Physical exercise can help you unwind and sleep better.

End of the day:

Looking back at my day, has there been a healthy balance between exercise, eating, relationships, rest, fun and jobs? Do I need to make an adjustment for tomorrow?

_____

_____

_____

_____

Which four people are bringing me joy at the moment? Why am I grateful to have them in my life?

_____

_____

_____

_____

Exercise is a celebration of what your body can do. Not a punishment for what you ate.
Unknown

https://www.facebook.com/groups/preventingteacherburnout

Friday

Date:_____

First thing:

How does my mind feel this morning? Would I describe it as cluttered, calm, anxious….other? Explain:

_____

_____

_____

What is one thing I could change in my home today that would bring me more peace?

_____

_____

_____

Tip: Ask yourself, "Is this a job I need to do? Is this an item I want to keep?"

End of the day:

What is my favourite space in my home? Why?

_____

_____

_____

_____

Tomorrow, which space could I spend a few minutes sorting so I have another favourite space?

_____

_____

_____

_____

Your home should tell the story of who you are, and be a
collection of what you love.
Nate Berkus

https://www.facebook.com/groups/preventingteacherburnout

Weekend

Date:_____

Rowena Hicks

First thing:

What are the three most important things for me to do this weekend to bring me and those I love joy?

_____

_____

_____

What are two things that I'm worrying about this morning? Can I control them? Is there a small step that I can take that would reduce my stress?

_____

_____

_____

Tip: Embrace the present and let go of what you can't control.

End of the day:

How am I doing with letting go of the things that I can't control, aren't really my problem or that I can delegate or speak to someone else about?

_____

_____

_____

_____

What has been my favourite memory from this week? Describe it in detail:

_____

_____

_____

_____

*The ability to be in the present moment is a major
component of mental wellness.*
Abraham Maslow

H, FLOURISH,
THRIVE

https://www.facebook.com/groups/preventingteacherburnout

WEEK - 51

WRITING A NEW STORY FOR MYSELF!

Monday

Date:_____

First thing:

What are three things I'm most grateful for in my life?

_____

_____

_____

_____

What are the main sources of my stress? How do I feel after writing them down and acknowledging them here?

_____

_____

_____

Tip: Taking a moment to invest in yourself is a first step to healing.

End of the day:

As I identify my top worries, what are a couple of small steps I can take towards addressing these? Can I make this a priority?

_____

_____

_____

_____

What went really well today? Describe it in detail:

_____

_____

_____

_____

You don't have to see the whole staircase, just take the first step.
Martin Luther King Jr.

https://www.facebook.com/groups/preventingteacherburnout

Tuesday

Date:_____

First thing:

Create a mantra that reminds me of my strength, like "I am resilient and capable."

_____

_____

_____

_____

What is an example of a time I faced adversity and I overcame it? How did I manage it?

_____

_____

_____

Tip: Do I expect more of myself than I can manage?

End of the day:

List three of my strengths that I have used to be able to flourish or overcome today:

_____

_____

_____

_____

What was my best moment today? Why was is so amazing?

_____

_____

_____

_____

Start where you are. Use what you have. Do what you can.
Arthur Ashe

https://www.facebook.com/groups/preventingteacherburnout

Wednesday

Date:_____

First thing:

Write down qualities I love about myself. Reflect on how these qualities contribute to my life and the lives of others:

_____

_____

_____

Now write down three more…just for me to see, it's not pride, it's recognising why I am indeed GOOD ENOUGH. I contribute so much:

_____

_____

_____

 Tip: You are good enough!

End of the day:

Write a time when I helped a friend or colleague overcome or sort out a situation that was really difficult:

_____

_____

_____

_____

How does my body feel today? Have I had some moments in which I've taken care of myself? Some self-compassion time? When? Do I need more tomorrow?

_____

_____

_____

_____

70% of people feel more empowered when they engage in self-affirmations (Psychology Today).

Thursday

Date:_____

First thing:

Take a moment to write about something I did recently that I initially thought I couldn't manage. How did I overcome?

_____

_____

_____

Visualise myself successfully completing a task that's on my list. Write about the positive outcomes that will follow:

_____

_____

_____

Tip: Set a small, achievable goal today and work towards it.

End of the day:

List three things I am pleased to have achieved today:

_____

_____

_____

_____

Who do I have in my life who is a cheerleader for me? How does this make me feel?

_____

_____

_____

_____

People who journal daily achieve 60% more of their goals than those who do not (Dominican University study).

https://www.facebook.com/groups/preventingteacherburnout

Friday

Date:_____

First thing:

What are my three main priorities right now? Are these for me or others?

_____

_____

_____

_____

What am I looking forward to most today and why?

_____

_____

_____

_____

Tip: See yourself as a bud that is becoming a beautiful flower.

End of the day:

If I see myself in a year, where do I want to be? Do I need to take a small step to make this more likely to happen? Am I excited by this idea?

_____

_____

_____

Can I tell myself that my potential is endless? Do I believe it? Can I write my own affirmation here?

_____

_____

_____

In the shaking and the pain, we find the next best level of ourselves.
Rowena Hicks

Buy My Book Here: www.rowenahicks.com/books

365

Weekend

Date:_____

First thing:

What do I feel I am growing in at the moment?

_____
_____
_____

What is an area around me where I can see potential opportunities?
How can I turn this potential into a reality? Does this idea excite me? Do
I have the courage to pursue it?

_____
_____
_____

**Tip: Believe in your limitless potential and the incredible things you
are capable of achieving.**

End of the day:

Acknowledging we all need to spend time doing things that make us feel
alive - what makes me feel alive at the moment?

_____
_____
_____
_____

What has been my biggest takeaway from this week?

_____
_____
_____

When exhausted, having a project you believe in is energising.
Rowena Hicks

Buy My Book Here: www.rowenahicks.com/books

WEEK - 52
WHAT I'VE LEARNT.....SO FAR!

Monday

Date:_____

First thing:

What are three things I've learnt through journaling? What is their impact on me?

_____

_____

_____

_____

What wound has been transferred to wisdom in my life recently?

_____

_____

_____

Tip: Even the smallest positive change we recognise contributes to creating our best selves.

End of the day:

What is a change I have made, or a small habit changed, as a result of journaling?

_____

_____

_____

_____

What has been my key win from today?

_____

_____

_____

_____

Turn your wounds into wisdom.
Oprah Winfrey

Tuesday

Date:_____

First thing:

Who am I grateful for in my life? How can I let them know?

_____

_____

_____

Can I identify areas of growth over the past year? Which am I most proud of?

_____

_____

_____

Tip: Take time to reflect to discover the fullness of your growth journey.

End of the day:

Is there one area for growth that I've been putting off? Maybe it's out of my comfort zone? Can I write it here, maybe even take a small step forward?

_____

_____

_____

_____

Have I had any moments today of self-care? What do these look like for me and what works best? Is it enough?

_____

_____

_____

_____

Without continual growth and progress, such words as improvement, achievement, and success have no meaning.
Benjamin Franklin

https://www.facebook.com/groups/preventingteacherburnout

Wednesday

Date:_____

First thing:

How is my body today? Relaxed or on high alert? What works to relax my mind and body?

_____

_____

_____

Who are the safe people in my life right now? Who could I ask for feedback on where I have achieved growth?

_____

_____

_____

Tip: Accept that everyone has areas in which they can grow and acknowledging them is the first step toward improvement.

End of the day:

Identify at least two areas where I feel I could improve. Then reflect on why they are important:

_____

_____

_____

_____

Can I give myself feedback on my day? Best moment and one I might improve next time?

_____

_____

_____

_____

We all need people who will give us feedback. That's how we improve.
Bill Gates

Thursday

Date:_____

First thing:

How is my self-talk this morning? Can I write myself a positive affirmation to start my day? Look in the back of the book for examples of affirmations:

_____

_____

_____

Do I have a long-term and short-term goal that are important to me?

_____

_____

_____

Tip: Focus on your next steps and how you will implement them to continue your journey of growth.

End of the day:

What is an action step I can take this week in order to move towards achieving one of my goals?

_____

_____

_____

_____

How is my sleep routine? How is my sleep? Is there one thing I can change to improve it?

_____

_____

_____

The first step towards getting somewhere is to decide you're not going to stay where you are.
J.P. Morgan

https://www.facebook.com/groups/preventingteacherburnout

Friday

Date:_____

First thing:

What is an area that I feel a bit stuck in? How can I raise the bar? Do I need training? Support? Something else?

_____

_____

_____

List some achievements from recent months that I am proud of:

_____

_____

_____

Tip: Listing what we got right pushes out our focus on what went wrong.

End of the day:

What are three small achievements from today? Nothing is too small.

_____

_____

_____

_____

Have I achieved a better ability to rest? What does rest look like for me? Have I learnt to prioritise it yet or is this a journey I need to take another action step on?

_____

_____

_____

_____

Celebrate what you've accomplished, but raise the bar a little higher
each time you succeed.
Mia Hamm

https://www.facebook.com/groups/preventingteacherburnout

Weekend

Rowena Hicks

Date:_____

First thing:

What three things am I most looking forward to this weekend?

_____

_____

_____

_____

What are two intentions I have for the coming weeks? What are the associated actions I need to take?

_____

_____

_____

Tip: You are enough! You are amazing! Just as you are!

End of the day:

If I see myself in three months time, what do I want to see I have changed?

_____

_____

_____

_____

What five positive and affirming words do I use to describe me now?

Can I stick these on my fridge?

I am:

_____

_____

_____

_____

Your life does not get better by chance; it gets better by change.
Jim Rohn

https://www.facebook.com/groups/preventingteacherburnout

FLOURISH, THRIVE

BONUS PAGES

GO TO THESE WHENEVER YOU NEED THEM:

AFFIRMATIONS

to remind you who you really are

 I am making a difference every day.

 I matter.

 Each day is a new opportunity to inspire and be inspired.

 I am stronger than I think.

 I am capable, confident, and committed.

 I may fail but I can get up again and grow.

 I bring joy.

 I am proud of the work I do and the impact I make.

AFFIRMATIONS
to remind you who you really are

 I am enough.

 Unless I take care of myself I can't help others.

 I am an important role model for those around me.

 I have value just as I am.

 I accept I am learning every day.

 I forgive myself.

 I am grateful for so much.

 I am not alone; I have a support system to lean on.

Identify how you feel today using emojis
How am I feeling?
Circle as many as you like or draw you own!

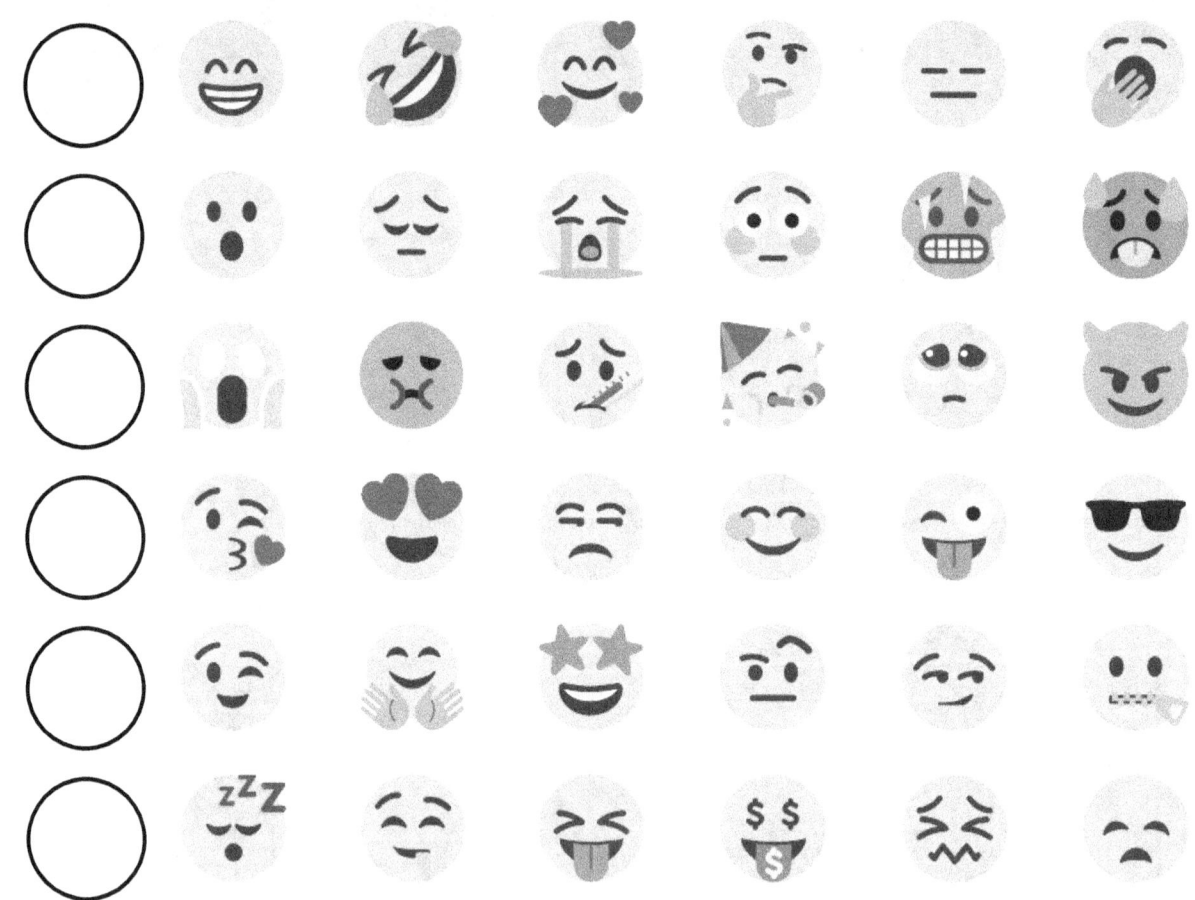

Beach
BUCKET LIST

For Example:
- Swim with dolphins!
- Make a life size sand castle!
- Have a sunset BBQ!

DREAM JAR!

7 floor house

Have 10 dogs   Meet Tom cruise

Beach house in Fiji

EMPATHETIC

Loved

COMPASSIONATE

INSPIRING

Enough

Valued

amazing

Special

Selfless

ENCOURAGING

NEEDED

kind

RADIANT

Gifted

loving

3 EXTRA INDIVIDUAL JOURNAL DAYS

WHEN YOU NEED SOMETHING MORE

Bonus Sheet 1

Date:_____

Weekend backup Journal sheet - or when I have just had
ONE OF THOSE DAYS!

First thing:

What would 20 minutes of quality self-care look like today for me?

_____

_____

_____

<u>S</u>tep 1 - plan it in! How?

_____

_____

E.g. Coffee with a friend / turn off my phone / my favorite hobby / bubble bath / power nap / read my book / go for a walk / cook my favorite food / buy myself a treat / other!

Step 2 - DO IT! Don't let it slip!

Step 3 - How did it feel to take a little control in my day?

_____

_____

_____

_____

Top tip - Just Do it!

How many things can I list that I am grateful for right now?

_____

_____

_____

_____

_____

_____

You've survived this far. You've got this!
Rowena Hicks

Buy My Book Here: www.rowenahicks.com/books

Bonus Sheet 2

Rowena Hick

Date:_____

Weekend backup Journal sheet - or when I have just need to remember you matter too!

First thing:

What are three things I love most about teaching?

_____

_____

_____

As I take a moment now, even in the rush of the start of the day, take five minutes to breathe. Notice how my body feels. Relax my muscles - face, shoulders, tongue, toes, everywhere! How am I?

_____

_____

_____

_____

Tip: Slow down! Even making the difference to one person today makes the day worth it. A smile? A kind word? Make them a coffee?

Who did I impact today? How did I help and what difference did I make?

_____

_____

_____

_____

How many things can I list that I am grateful for right now?

_____

_____

_____

_____

You owe yourself the love that you so freely give to other people.
Unknown

https://www.facebook.com/groups/preventingteacherburnout

TEACH, FLOURISH, THRIVE

Bonus Sheet 3

Date:_____

Weekend backup Journal sheet – time for a gratitude review!

First thing:

1. Create a list of gratitude prompts related to different aspects of life, such as nature, relationships, personal achievements, or simple pleasures, even areas of school that I am grateful for:

_____

_____

_____

2. As I find things, describe them - even if it is small:

_____

_____

_____

_____

Tip: Gratitude has been linked to better sleep, reduced stress, and even lower blood pressure.

At the end of today, have I started noticing more of the things I am grateful for or the things and people I am grateful for?

_____

_____

_____

_____

3. Was this a worthwhile reflection? How has it helped my outlook?

_____

_____

_____

_____

When you are grateful, fear disappears and abundance appears.
Tony Robbins

https://www.facebook.com/groups/preventingteacherburnout

LIFE PLANNER EXAMPLES

TRY IT TO PUT YOUR NEEDS FIRST

Welcome to The Teacher Experience 'Life' planner every teacher needs. Each slot is a dedicated hour but this template can be adapted to work for you! We have included some examples of how we get the planner to work for us, just in case you needed some scaffolding. To find out more about everything teaching, listen to The Teacher Experience Podcast on Spotify, Amazon or YouTube and follow us on Instagram @theteacherexperience24

Spotify

Miss Wylde's Life Planner

	Monday	Tuesday	Wednesday	Thursday	Friday	Saturday	Sunday
Pre-School				Gym			
Pre-School	High cognitive tasks / Morning briefing @8:15	High cognitive tasks / marking	High cognitive tasks / marking	High cognitive tasks / marking	High cognitive tasks / marking	Sleep and Gym	
Tutor	Teaching	Teaching	Teaching	Teaching	Teaching		
Period 1	Teaching	Teaching	Teaching	PPA - Admin	Teaching	1 Hour Passion Project	
Period 2	Teaching	Teaching	Teaching	Teaching	Teaching		
Break	Tea and Snack	Tea and Snack	Tea and Snack	Tea and Snack	Tea and Snack	1 Hour Training Course	
Period 3	Teaching	Teaching	Teaching	Teaching	PPA - Requisition		
Lunch Duty	Canteen Entrance	Canteen Entrance	Canteen Entrance	Canteen Entrance	Canteen Entrance	Prioritise:	
Period 4	Teaching	PPA - Admin	Meet ECT 'C'	Teaching	Meet ECT 'M'		
Period 5	Teaching	Teaching	Teaching	PPA - Admin	Teaching	Friends and Family	
Post-School	CPD	Low Cognitive Tasks	Low Cognitive Tasks	Low Cognitive Tasks - Leave ASAP	Low Cognitive Tasks - Leave ASAP	Good Food	
Post-School	Low Cognitive Tasks	Low Cognitive Tasks	Low Cognitive Tasks	Date Night	Gym	Relaxing	
Post-School	Gym	Gym	Gym	Date Night			
Post-School		Passion Project				Remember... it can wait	

CH, FLOURISH, THRIVE

Mrs Dearman's Life Planner							
	Monday	Tuesday	Wednesday	Thursday	Friday	Saturday	Sunday
Before School	Set all homework's for the week	Coffee with Science Team	Plan Science Practical's for next week	Mark books or homework	Morning Briefing		
P1		Teaching	Teaching	Teaching	Teaching		
P2	Teaching	Teaching	Teaching	Mark books or homework			
P3	Teaching	Teaching		Teaching	Teaching		
P3	Teaching		Teaching	Teaching			
Lunch	30 minute walk	30 minute walk	30 minute walk	30 minute walk	30 minute walk		
P4			Teaching	Mark books or homework			
P5	Teaching	Teaching	Teaching	Teaching	Teaching		
P6		Teaching	SENCo Meeting	Mark books or homework	Teaching		
After School	School Meeting	Print Worksheets for Wednesday Leave by 4:30pm	Print Worksheets for Thursday Leave by 4:30pm	Print Worksheets for Friday Leave by 4:30pm	Print Worksheets for Monday Leave by 4:30pm		
Me time	Evening Walk	Gym Running	Evening Walk	Date Night	Pub with the Team	Gym – Cycle	Gym – Strength

Template							
	Monday	Tuesday	Wednesday	Thursday	Friday	Saturday	Sunday

EXTRA BLANK SHEETS

TO WRITE WHEN YOU NEED MORE SPACE.

https://linktr.ee/authorrowenahicks

Amazon Best Sellers

Our most popular products based on sales. Updated frequently.

Best Sellers in Psychological Education & Training

Top 100 Paid   Top 100 Free

Teach, Flourish, Thrive: Break Free From...
› Rowena Hicks
★★★★★ 8
Kindle Edition
£0.99

Buy the Book here:

SCAN ME

For more information, go to www.rowenahicks.com

www.ingramcontent.com/pod-product-compliance
Lightning Source LLC
Chambersburg PA
CBHW080849120626
46546CB00008B/2749